NEAR DEATH
NEAR LIFE

A JOURNEY INTO THE MYSTIC

By Andrew Zorich

The events and conversations in this book have been set down to the best of the author's ability, although some names, details, and locations have been changed to protect the privacy of individuals.

This book is not intended as a substitute for the medical advice of physicians. The reader should regularly consult a physician in matters relating to his/her health and particularly with respect to any symptoms that may require diagnosis or medical attention.

ISBN: 978-1-7351557-3-9

Edits and layout: Liz Carleton

www.DiamondBodywork.com/book

CONTENTS

DEDICATION

To Corvin, my joy.
To Erika, my bliss.
The Universe cannot contain my love for you both.

INTRODUCTION

This book is a reflection on my exploration of the meditative and intuitive healing arts. It begins in my youth, and as the story twists and turns it lays out a journey of self-healing and transformation. The book is layered, each chapter building upon the previous, creating an energetic road map of sorts. The teachings and techniques that I learned are multilayered and multifaceted, containing many universal applications. It is a true story with some character names and details adjusted to protect identities. My deeper intent for this book is to provide a glimpse of the beauty of the work that was gifted to me, while my hope is that it serves as a reminder that we are inherently magical beings with incredible untapped possibilities.

CHAPTER ONE
EVERYTHING AND NOTHING

When I was 18, the experience of cloudiness in the sky was common. My shoes were often navigating a shiny layer of rain-water on the Seattle sidewalks. It was normal for me to wander the streets, the noise of traffic an ever-present ocean rumble in the background. I lived in a small Capitol Hill apartment, while my second home was a coffee shop on the corner of Melrose and Pine.

I would order my coffee, a double latte, and a pack of American Spirit cigarettes. Wandering upstairs, I would find a seat in the dark, smoky second floor. Morrisey or some other moody artist would be playing over the speakers. I would sit in a quiet corner where I could do my art while people-watching. I would pull out my large drawing pad; just another day of writing poetry or drawing something obscure. It didn't matter; there was never a time when I was not immersed in my art. The pencil translated my feelings – often some angst turned into pictures, some grief turned into words – while the coffee was my liquid energy.

Eventually, it was time for me to go to work. I would pack up and head to my downtown restaurant job, a popular and fast-paced place where I bussed dishes. I would put on the daily work role for a while, rushing dishes to the back of the kitchen in this fancy restaurant across from the Paramount Hotel. The bosses loved me. I worked hard, harder than most. I gave it my all and the waiters and waitresses would respond with big tips. The bigger the tips, the more money I had for coffee and cigarettes.

These were my days, living in the heart of the city, driven by caffeine with no rhyme or reason. If I had a day off my friends knew where to find me, with my head sunk into my drawing pad.

Though this mellow lifestyle outwardly appeared easy, it was unsettled, and the underlying mood I often felt was one of discomfort. Each day the darkness of the cloudy city would engulf me a tiny bit more. Each day the smoke from those cigarettes would sink a little deeper. Each day the coffee became less a pleasure and more of a need. Each day I began to sink deeper into my art in a way that gave no escape, darkness enveloping my attitude, slowly absorbing any childlike joy I carried inside me.

* * *

When I was a child, I would have occasional pains in my abdomen, at random times a sharp, stabbing pain that would pierce through my body. Brief but painful, these pains would occur when I was falling asleep or relaxing, alone, and quiet with my thoughts. They would appear and then, just as mysteriously, disappear. The pain would always follow with a deep sense of grief, an unknown but real pang of childlike sadness. There was always a feeling that the grief was connected to a deeper part of me, an unknown part of me longing for something that I could not touch or reach.

* * *

It was just another night. I got home late from my restaurant job. I was pretty tired, so I went straight into my bedroom to sleep. Suddenly the familiar pains in my stomach appeared. I bent slightly over, holding onto my lower abdomen with both hands. The pains were particularly painful this time, and rather than lasting for a short duration they didn't go away. Something was different this time as the pain increased. The stabbing slowly became searing, shooting to the core of my body causing me to bend over, so intense that I eventually curled up in a ball on the floor. In that moment of increased pressure and pain, I somehow knew to the very core of my being that I was about to die. I just knew with every cell that this was the end. As this experience increased the realization came that I had not lived – I had not truly lived. I began to cry. In the fetal position on the floor waves of deep grief washed through me, pain increasing, and pressure bearing down.

This unbelievable pressure continued to increase, building and building and building until I unconsciously called, "I don't want to die today! I will do anything! I will do anything!"

In that instant, as if in response to my call, a lightning bolt of light struck through me and I exploded across the Universe. My entire being shattered into a million pieces and I was gone. I had dissolved entirely into the fullness and emptiness of the Universe. I was space, a pure space of all that is, a space beyond form, beyond light, with only a feeling of endless pure love. In this place, I was there, but with no body and no thought… a space of clearer-than-clear light, clearer than the clearest awareness.

In this experience, I heard a voice. "You are everything… You are nothing… And you are the light beyond that… The Universe is everything… The Universe is nothing… And it is the light beyond that. There is no separation between... You are pure, untainted love, and the Universe is pure, untainted love. There is no division between you and all of creation. Fear is the only division... Fear is the only illusion..."

I not only heard these words but felt them and experienced them fully as resonant truth in that moment. I experienced myself as pure, unending love. I was one with all that is and all who are.

The next moment, I was above my body looking at myself curled up on the floor. As I approached my body, I could see that I was no longer crying but laughing. I had no idea how much time had passed, maybe hours, maybe seconds, but as I descended into my body, I was laughing a childlike laughter. I was laughing at how seriously I had taken my life, at all the fear and control I tried to have over my reality. This illusion, this pseudo-boundary between myself and all things, was a literal cosmic joke. There was no doubt in my mind at that moment that I was pure love; that all beings were endless, pure love; and that this pure, clearer-than-clear love existed as ever-present nowness within everything.

As I fully came back down to reality the pain in my abdomen had completely disappeared and has since never returned. I felt a sense of calm, a sense of ease, a sense of unspoiled love. I felt truly free. After arriving back down on planet Earth all I knew was that I was supposed to be a warrior of love, of clear love. What being a warrior of love looked like in my life, I had no idea.

This experience changed me. I went back to my daily routine – work, coffee shop, smoking, and living through the same bodily actions I had before. Yet, there had been a monumental shift. This shift didn't just bring with it inner awareness; it also brought with it physical perceptual shifts. Things didn't look the same.

It started when I was sitting in my usual coffee shop spot, people-watching as they walked by. As I watched them, they started to exude a glow with varied colors. At first, it was in my peripheral vision and I thought maybe there was something wrong with me, something wrong with my eyes, so I rubbed them. But as I focused on it, I began to see these glowing energies all around many people. The more I focused on them the brighter they became, and eventually I began seeing these colors in my direct vision.

Sometimes the glowing would be around the forms of people, like an aura, and sometimes their faces would change color and shape, a sort of glowing mask of varied colors. If I looked long enough at someone it would get more intense and the visual would morph and change, like a moving face on top of their physical face. Some would seem darker than others and if I saw a darker or angrier face, I would often avoid that person. Occasionally a snake-like face would give me an intuition to be careful around the person.

There was an issue though with this newfound perceptual experience: the more I focused on people's glowing energy, the more tired I slowly started to feel. It was as if it zapped all my physical energy. I became so fascinated and absorbed with these auras and energies but it would wear me out and make me feel deeply tired, which indicated something was slightly wrong – yet my fascination outweighed the tiredness and so I kept at it often.

Beyond the perception shifts, I also had intuitions that appeared while talking with people. I just knew things. There were times when I knew people were lying and times when I might add to a conversation something I could not know. It was often unorganized and random, but it was a clear shift in me since the near-death experience and it would catch people off guard. I sometimes would just tell people they were lying to me without knowing why, and they would look shocked and admit it.

In the beginning, right after my near-death expansion, I felt a sense of deep love all the time, as though I was continually connected to that beautiful space. During that time, the world felt right, and I had a deep meaning in my life, but as time slowly passed and as the normal day-to-day life patterns continued, that feeling of love lingered less and less. If I focused hard on the near-death experience, I could bring myself back to that positive feeling, but because I often found myself around the familiar faces before my experience, it started to dissipate.

Of the people that I shared my experience with, many did not understand what I had gone through and most people were very negative about my experience. The familiar people I spent time with were not that loving and with my perceptual shifts, it magnified the fact that I was very alone in my view and my experience of the world. Not one person I knew understood or even wanted to understand what I had gone through. Some looked at me like I was crazy, and some could not even hear what I was saying.

Eventually, I stopped talking about it. Slowly, over time, it felt like darkness was creeping in and I felt like I was being slowly sucked into a hole of forced ignorance and forced quietness. This, mixed with the feeling of love disappearing, caused me to be subsumed by inner frustration and bitterness, which were reflected in my art, my attitude, and my outlook on life. I needed help.

CHAPTER TWO
THE DOORWAY

On a day off I was wandering a street called Broadway, a few blocks from where I lived. This particular day I noticed a small alleyway that I hadn't seen before, with little shops that lined each side. As I wandered into this alley there appeared some steps that led to an upper section of businesses. I looked up to see a silver-haired man leaning on the railing staring down at me. For a moment I was a little taken aback as I paused and locked eyes with him. There was no expression from this man – just a piercing gaze that caught me off guard and lasted for an inordinate amount of time. After a while, he walked away. I continued exploring the shops and eventually headed up the stairs. I looked around to see a tattoo shop on one side and a bookstore called The Sage on the other. This aroused my interest and I walked inside. As I looked around there were all sorts of crystals and other New Age objects, and I could see a little chart with a price for astrology readings. I went to the counter, which was situated in a little corner, to ask about these readings and the silver-haired man was sitting there. He didn't say anything; he just stared at me, almost as if he were looking through me. I asked him about the readings.

"Oh, I'm sorry. The owner who does astrology readings isn't here today. I do readings of a different kind," he said.

We began to talk and for some inexplicable reason, I found myself sharing my story with that man. I told him that I had a near-death experience and how that event impacted my life. As I spoke his gaze seemed to get more piercing, and his eyes began to shine peculiarly.

He stood up and walked over to a chart hanging on the wall.

"It was like this, no?" He pointed to a circular chart showing layers of the human being in energetic and subtle form. I nodded.

He introduced himself and said his name was Mathias. He put his hand on my shoulder and said, "It's going to be all right now."

I looked at him with a bit of shock and awe as he somehow touched upon the deep pain I had been feeling that I wasn't acknowledging, the pain of losing the feeling of my near-death experience. I felt shaken up and comforted all at the same time. I didn't say anything else. I turned around and left, walking the small few city blocks down the hill to where I lived.

When I got to my front door I was in deep thought about Mathias and how that was such an interesting and odd conversation. While I was unlocking the door to my apartment, I heard a woman's voice behind me clearly say, "Tell him to teach you what he knows." I turned abruptly around to see who was there, but there was no one. The voice didn't scare me, but it left an impactful impression – I felt shocked with chills. Over the evening I couldn't shake the feeling and I knew that I needed to ask him to teach me whatever he knew.

The next day I followed the advice of the voice and walked into the alley and up the stairs. Mathias was standing there again, looking over the railing and staring piercingly at me like he was waiting for me. I walked right up to him and said quite abruptly, "Will you teach me what you know?"

Mathias looked surprised for a moment and then burst into laughter. He composed himself and looked above him as if analyzing something from above. His face then became very serious and his piercing gaze returned, almost as if he were staring through me. As if assessing some ethereal energy, he put his hand on my shoulder and said, "I do teach, and I only teach people who ask."

He began to laugh again like he was joking with someone. He then proceeded to say he was a teacher of healing, a teacher of the art of self-awareness. He said he was a teacher of tools to help a person with their ability to heal the inner wounds, to protect themselves, and to open their intuition to use it properly.

He looked at me seriously and said that if I chose this journey the opportunity would be up to me as to how far I would want to go with it. I was elated and wonderstruck that I had met someone who recognized my near-death experience and who taught things that could help me.

He looked at me seriously again and said, "There is something very important for you to understand right now." He put his hand on my back. "Being grounded on the earth is deeply important for you. You have been floating almost dangerously around, being pulled by things outside your body, and it is good to be in your body."

At that moment I felt a weight pull down on me as if gravity had become strong. I felt more solid in my body. I could recognize that I had not been in my body, especially while staring at all the visual experiences I had been having. Mathias was showing me something. His presence had made me feel heavier, like a weight was connected to my feet and as if gravity had become stronger.

He said, "Being in the body is very important, particularly for you."

He then looked off in space, and after staying quiet for a long pause he said, "That is enough information for today. Come back in a week."

Lost in amazement, I turned around and left.

Around a week later I went back. Again, he was standing next to the railing, overlooking the stairs. As I approached him, he had an eagle-like gaze. I couldn't discern his age; it could have been anywhere between late 30s to 70s. He was dressed in silvery grey pants and a silver button-up shirt. Both times I had met him I had not been able to discern his background.

He welcomed me this time with a big hug and patted my back. I noticed that in his presence I felt a strong sense of well-being, as though he exuded this feeling of well-being. The more time I spent with him the more I wanted to learn what he knew, what his secrets were. During this visit we stood at the top of stairs watching people from above, leaning on the railing.

As we talked, I told Mathias, "I feel I am ready to learn." He smirked and said, "Everything you need to know is already inside you. What I am going to teach you are just tools to get there."

Standing next to each other, we looked over the railing. He then said in a deep and calm voice, "Close your eyes."

"Take a deep breath and relax. Imagine yourself breathing in light with every inhale. Breathe light into every cell of your body and then breathe out all of your tension." He guided my breath deeper.

"Imagine a time you felt deeply loved, and imagine that love becoming a light inside you. Let it build and expand and become more and more brilliant. See that beautiful light shoot above you into the Universe above and allow the love of the Universe above to return that light but even brighter, a beautiful white light filling your entire being. Fill yourself with this light and when you feel full, truly full of this beautiful light, just pour all the excess below you into the earth. Allow that light to flow to the center of the earth and allow that love to return to you in a deeply grounding and powerfully nurturing light. As you love the earth, the earth returns your love manifold in a beautiful golden light."

He continued, "See these two loops of light between the Universe above and the grounding earth below, connect them, and see a figure 8 of infinity within you. See this brilliant light between the earth and the Universe. Be in this space of infinite light. Know you are infinite light. You can come back to this place of love within yourself at any time."

He said that I could open my eyes when I was ready.

I had gone so deep within myself. I was amazed by how deep I went in a public space. Everything had disappeared but my inner experience. The power and love of this experience was profound. I felt different, grounded, and strong.

Mathias said that that was enough for today and told me to practice what he had shared and come back when I was ready.

I went home and spent every available moment closing my eyes and connecting to this new experience of filling myself with light and love from above and below. For the first time since my near-death experience, I felt as if I were connected to something grander and that I was not alone. I would feel all the darkness and tension melt out of me daily.

I returned to The Sage not too long after, eager for what was next. Mathias was there staring piercingly at me, in the same spot, as if he were expecting me.

This time he looked at me seriously and said, "There is a responsibility with this work we are going to be doing. When you take responsibility for yourself and your energy you become more respectful of other people, not just in physical interaction but in energy. You become a responsible, energetic being. This responsibility creates power within you and helps you maintain your inner stability."

Standing next to me, both of us looking over the ledge, he said, "Close your eyes, and take a deep breath. Slowly start to breathe in light and love and allow yourself to breathe out any tension. As you breathe, move your focus to the very center of your head, to the area of the pineal gland, what some call the third eye, located in the very center of your head."

"Now imagine love building inside you... Feel a love build and see that love become light... Send that light above you to the Universe above and receive the beautiful light in return. Let the light and love of the Universe fill you. As you love, so you are loved. See a loop forming between you and the Universe above. Now send that love below you to the center of the earth. Feel the earth respond with a beautiful grounding light. Feel how you are loved by the earth and feel how you are filled with a strong and healing grounding light. Now see the two loops connect into the symbol of infinity: the earth below and the Universe above. See yourself connected and strong, a being of light and energy."

"Now centering in your third eye I want you to see a screen, like a movie screen. This screen is like a filter to help focus the information that is going to come through your third eye, through your intuitive center." He paused for a while as I explored inside myself with this screen.

He then continued, "For a moment see yourself on this screen; notice if you can see yourself. Attempt to see your whole body on this screen and then allow yourself to see the energy around your body… Just notice things; just notice what you see."

At first, I only saw a portion of my body appear. As I relaxed and allowed a little more, I noticed that my whole body appeared. As it appeared, I saw streams of energy coming from all around my body, orange in some areas, white in others, some red below, and some black on my right.

He then said, "I want you to imagine you have a paintbrush of light and I want you to see yourself brighten up your energy field with this paintbrush. See any dark spots and brighten them up, making each area as bright as you can. Maybe some spots don't brighten as much as you would like, and that's okay. You can work on it more and more anytime."

Mathias continued, "It's time to clear your screen. Allow your screen to become blank as if you were blinking your third eye, clearing off any images, back to a clear and empty screen. Clearing the screen will clear any unwanted energy.

"Now it's time to come back out of this meditation and slowly, slowly open your eyes when you're ready."

I opened my eyes feeling so good; my energy had shifted, particularly the areas I went over with my paintbrush. Mathias smiled and said, "Now you have something to play with when you get home. Spend some time practicing this and come back soon."

* * *

The next time I visited Mathias I felt ready to move forward. I had practiced and I was energized for my next lesson. I couldn't get enough of this newfound experience.

Mathias was in his normal place looking as if he had been waiting for me. Each time I visited him it felt like time had stopped and we would pick up right where we had left off.

This time he said, "Even though we may see things outside ourselves, we should work not to get lost in the fascination with those things. External pulls can be draining for some people." He gave me a funny look hinting that he was talking about me, making me laugh.

He pointed to his heart and said, "What is important is on the inside."

I started sharing with him more about things I had seen and experienced after my near-death experience. He explained that he felt I was seeing people's masks, their underlying faces. People may look one way on the outside, but he surmised that I was seeing a more underlying emotional expression. He explained that even though I was having these experiences, they were more fascinating than helpful. He mentioned that the outside is fleeting. I told him I felt tired if I followed the energy visually.

He said, "It is safer to use the inner world to explore intuition. Sometimes we look for proof of our experience in outside experiences, and underlying the surface are all sorts of deep-rooted issues that are driving our fascinations, both in the psychic and physical worlds. These fascinations can encompass all areas of life."

His eyes then got piercing and he said, "Sometimes we are looking for power..." He stayed quiet for a long time.

I went home and thought about what Mathias had been saying. I realized that my work and lifestyle had shifted since starting to meditate. I found it shocking and amazing that since the day I met Mathias I had stopped smoking and I rarely entered the coffee shop that used to be a home base. I spent more and more time meditating at home with the tools he had given me. Though they seemed somewhat simple they opened up whole realms of experiences within me. The more I meditated the more I wanted to learn, so I went back to see him again and again.

* * *

One day Mathias said, "Let's go for a walk."

We walked along a busy street and Mathias seemed to know everyone; people smiled and said hi to him all over the busy street.

He said to me, "Intention is everything... Let's go into this coffee shop."

We walked in and he said, "Go ahead of me and order."

I ordered a coffee, and then Mathias stood at the counter. The man behind the counter gave me my coffee but didn't ask for Mathias's order. Mathias just stood there with a glint in his eye. The man seemed to look everywhere, but not at Mathias who had been standing right in front of him for a long time. It became increasingly uncomfortable watching the man ignore Mathias.

With a glint in his eye, Mathias smirked at me and said, "Let's go."

I was confused. Was Mathias mad at the barista? Why didn't the barista take his order? He didn't even look at him!

We walked quietly back to the alleyway and up the stairs. We leaned against the railing like usual, looking down over the alley. I asked, "Did you not want coffee?"

The glint in Mathias's eyes still shining, "I didn't want a coffee. I was showing you intention."

He then said, "Close your eyes. Take a deep breath, breathing in light and love and connecting inside."

I felt all the nervous energy flow out of me, and I could feel Mathias energy-assisting in this process.

He continued, "Center in the center of your mind, your third eye. Send your light and love above you and below you; see your third eye screen and allow your body to come up on that screen. Correct your energy with your light brush and now... surround yourself with a beautiful bubble of light, a healing bubble that keeps your energy contained and protects you, healing you constantly. He paused.

"Now... Imagine a silvery liquid pouring over this white bubble. When this silvery liquid pours over the bubble it forms into a mirror... This is a mirror of reflection and a mirror of invisibility. This mirror is a wonderful place if you want to be invisible or want to take a break from big crowds. Notice the shift in you when wearing this mirror." He then said, "Slowly come out the meditation."

He smiled. Everything seemed brighter to me when we would do these small meditations.

We stayed quiet for a while and then he smiled and said, "I gave you an example of my intention when we walked into the coffee shop. Intention is a way of being not a forced action. I showed you a way of being invisible with the mirror in the coffee shop."

He continued, "Everything is a mirror for us, and placing a mirror around us will magnify this experience of a mirrored reality. It is simply an intention. It also will help contain your energy if you feel you are all over the place with your energy."

He asked if I understood what he meant by intention.

I said, "Not exactly."

He responded, "If you force the energy like this…" and he made a hilarious squished face. "It's like being constipated." He laughed. "But when you use intention there is no force. It happens; it is something higher. It is the simplest and yet most subtle experience." He paused, looking at me.

"Practice and meet me in a couple of weeks at the Arboretum." He gave me directions to a certain part of the park. He said to be very careful not to use the mirror crossing streets or near cars.

I practiced and practiced. I spent every available minute sitting in meditation or taking a break at work connecting to the energy.

Two weeks later I went to the park where Mathias had told me to meet him. He was sitting on a bench under a maple tree that was changing into fall colors. Mathias had two little dogs with him, one all white and one all black.

Both dogs barked loudly at me as I approached. Petting them he said, "This is Luciano, and this is Vincente." He said, "They won't bite, that I know of," and he laughed. I sat down, but they were still barking.

He said, "They are very sensitive… animals are very sensitive. Are you connected to the earth? Do you feel like you are in your body?"

I had not been paying attention, so I took a deep breath and sent energy to the earth and felt myself sink deeper into my body.

As I did this, the dogs stopped barking.

Mathias smiled and said, "These two have been with me for a long time. They are rescue dogs; they are a lot like me."

I wondered what he meant by that. I petted them and they both just stared at me, both with a glow in their eyes I hadn't seen dogs have before.

As if noticing what I was seeing Mathias said, "They help me with this work… Now we are going to do something a little different. Close your eyes and connect to your light systems. Connect to the light above and below. Feel the love building inside you."

I slowly connected. Then he said, "See the bubble of light around yourself and then see your third eye screen… And now on that screen, I want you to see Luciano."

I saw Luciano, and I saw his energy appear around him.

Mathias said, "Now let his energy be seen and notice what colors you see, or feel are coming from him. Ask Luciano on that screen if he is willing to receive healing and light from you. It is important to be respectful, always respectful, and always ask no matter what level we are working from."

I asked Luciano in the meditation and his energy gave me the impression that he was willing to receive healing.

"Now take your light brush and brighten any areas that seem dark or problematic."

Luciano's energy was already a bright white, but I attempted to brighten it up even more. I felt him relax a little.

Mathias continued, "Now talk to Luciano on this level and see if he has anything he wants to relay."

I heard Luciano say, "I love my dad."

Mathias told me that I could come out of meditation after clearing my third eye screen. He was smiling, holding Luciano on his lap.

Mathias said, "People experience things differently inside themselves within their third eyes. Some people see things clearly like you, and some people feel things deeply, which can sometimes be uncomfortable when things aren't positive. Some people hear things, and some people smell things. These all overlap inside you, but some are more pronounced than others. The more you practice the stronger these awarenesses will increase."

I told Mathias that Luciano was very sweet, yet strong.

Mathias smiled and said, "Luciano and I are one."

At this point, I interrupted and asked him something I had been wondering. "Where do these teachings come from?"

He paused and looked into the distance. He said, "Each person's lessons are different and so the teachings and tools are specific to the individual. Some tools are passed from teacher to student, but some come directly from Spirit. My mentor's name was Nikki, and, in a way, she nursed me back to health."

His eyes seemed to get a bit glossy. "When I was a child, I was put in the foster care system and in that system, I suffered a lot."

He said that at one time, at a very young age, he was thrown down a flight of stairs. As he lay mangled at the bottom of the stairs nearly lifeless, he came out of his body. As he looked down on himself, he committed to coming back into his body. He said, "I chose not to give up on life. Even though I should have died, my spirit decided to stay."

Due to this experience and others in his childhood, he carried a lot of trauma in his body that manifested as sickness and bodily dysfunction until he found this work. He said he healed himself with the help of Nikki and that the teachings were designed just for him by Spirit through his teacher and her experience. The result of this healing brought him to now work in the foster care system helping those who need his help.

He mentioned how everyone's path is different, and so their healing is manifested differently.

He looked at me and said, "It is up to the individual and Spirit how far and how much healing they are willing to do."

Then, staring at me seriously, his voice got a little louder. "You can gain any number of skills, and manifest any number of powers, but it is all pointless in the end if you have not healed your traumas. To reach infinity you must become clear." He then relaxed and smiled as if listening to someone speak to him subtly. He said, "We've just begun."

Mathias informed me that at the end of the following month he would be holding a class with another student and that I was welcome to join. I, of course, was on board. I was enthralled with this work and was ready to learn more. During the time in between, I meditated and practiced everything I had been shown so far as much as I could.

* * *

Around this same time, a coworker named Angela asked me if I had any interest in helping her move down to Los Angeles. I did not know her very well at the time, but she asked me as she had no one else to help. She particularly needed help driving the long distance from Seattle. I gladly accepted as I had never been to LA before.

We started our journey in a little Honda Civic towing a U-Haul trailer behind us. I kind of laughed to myself when I saw this tiny car. I thought to myself, "This is going to be an adventure." As we started our journey some music started to play on the radio. It was a famous band and Angela said she had grown up with these guys. She said that much of her teenage years were spent touring with them and that she ended up around a lot of famous musicians. Now she was a massage therapist and waitress and she was going to move in with a friend whom she had met during those many adventures touring with this band. She mentioned that this friend was a well-known music producer who also was a drummer in a famous band. She went on to say that he could be a bit moody. I said okay, thinking to myself, "Wow!" It was all very unexpected.

The drive was long and slow, especially over the hills of northern California. When we got to LA we drove into an industrial park. We pulled in front of a house that was strangely located with no other houses around it – set in the middle of industrial buildings. What made it even more odd was that the house had a small picket fence surrounding it.

Angela said, "We are here!"

The small house was surrounded by lots of tropical plants. I met the family and the man whose house it was. He seemed nice, but his face showed something heavy, with deep lines of life carved into it. As my friend settled in they all caught up. The owner of the house turned to tell me he was a recovering heroin addict, a constantly recovering heroin addict. This didn't impact me much but explained the pain in his eyes and the tension in his face.

The man told me that I could stay for a couple of weeks if I wanted, since I had not been to LA. I thanked him and took him up on the offer. As the days passed while I slept on their couch I would meditate in the morning and night. Something unsettling became prevalent inside me when I meditated but I couldn't put my finger on it. It seemed like an underlying awareness that I was there for a reason beyond helping Angela. I felt uneasy about the underlying feeling. The more I meditated, the more a pain that lived in the house became apparent. Interestingly each day more well-known music celebrities would pass through the home to go to the man's studio in the back. The more people I met, the more the underlying pressure built.

The music producer took a liking to me and it gave me a sense of excitement. At that moment I thought of my father and how this would be his dream come true. He was an actor, comedian, and singer. He was always struggling to get his next gig, always the life of the party, and he was always living with this intense desire to be liked by people. Underlying his dreams, he suffered from varied addictions in his life, which was part of his persona.

As a child I wanted to prove I was like my dad, singing in bands and acting in school. I wanted to show him I was great like him. Since my parents had separated when I was four, I always felt an intense need for his approval.

After a week of being in this house, the music producer offered to record me. It was as if all my childhood dreams of proving my abilities to my father my were unfolding. I saw how all my childhood dreams could come to fruition without me even showing the man I could sing! Yet, I could not shake the intuitive feeling that underlying all of this opportunity there was a pain, a deep, emotional, throbbing pain. When I mediated the pain became more and more obvious, like a throbbing headache. I could not ignore it.

By the second week of being surrounded by these famous people filtering in and out, I woke to a pristine awareness – like something had broken open inside of me, and I became pristinely aware that this was not the life that I was choosing for myself. This was the life of my father, his dreams, his desires, and his addictions. When this realization came to me, I sat in meditation, and it was as if a bright light moved and passed through me, vibrating, and lifting something deeply heavy off me, pulling out of my energy an entire life that wasn't mine. I felt free.

In meditation, the burden of my father's dreams was separated and cleared from me. This culminated in seeing myself as a child in a vision on my third eye screen, a child simply looking for love and acceptance. Seeing it helped this burden lift.

I thanked these people for their amazing hospitality and thanked them for the stay. I went home freed of a deep burden I had long carried. Some people might say it was a gift to be around some of the most famous musicians in the world, but I came away seeing the true gift, which was freedom from a prison I didn't even know I was living in. I now knew with clarity that I had my own life to live.

I came back to Seattle and I told Mathias about my experience. He didn't interrupt my long story.

After listening, he just smiled and said, "That sounds very healing."

I nodded yes and smiled back. For a moment I got a taste of the healing of this work and how the light is used to heal issues that underlie the surface.

CHAPTER THREE
MEDITATION

It was time for class. I had known Mathias for about a year, and I was excited to learn some new techniques. I arrived at Mathias's house. It was a light blue two-story home with a little wraparound yard. Luciano and Vincente greeted me at a short fence gate. They were staring at me, barking loudly from behind the fence. I laughed quietly to myself, thinking that I must be ungrounded. Mathias greeted me with a hug and told me to go around back to the sliding door, make myself at home, and have a seat on the couch. As I made myself comfortable, I felt a little anxious as I had no idea what we were going to learn.

The sliding door opened, and a woman walked in. She immediately shook my hand and said her name was Yuko. While holding my hand she said, "You are a very gentle soul."

A little taken aback, unsure how to respond, I smiled and thanked her.

Mathias came in and the dogs jumped up on the couch next to me and Yuko. Luciano, of course, sat next to me, staring at me with his shiny eyes and barking off and on. I focused on sending energy to the earth, and Luciano calmed down and curled up in a ball cozying up next to me as I grounded myself.

Mathias looked at me and Yuko and welcomed us. He said this was a class on awakening intuition and learning to use our energy in new ways. This was also an introduction to the power of self-healing.

We first did introductions. I told Yuko about how I had met Mathias near The Sage store and that I had started studying with him. Yuko said she was an educator for children on the autism spectrum and that she had always been very intuitive, especially when she was a child. She was hoping to explore this side of herself in the class.

Mathias then started the class by saying, "Let's meditate."

He took us to a familiar place, starting by breathing in light and breathing out tension; then breathing deeper and releasing even more tension.

He brought us to our third eyes and said, "Locate the feeling of your Source, the Source of you. Get a sense of the Source of you and feel it; feel the love and let it build, sending light and love to the Universe above and allowing it to cascade down into your being in a beautiful white light… Now send that same love deep into the earth, allowing the earth to love you in return with a strong and beautiful golden and grounding light. Feel this light healing you, making you strong and youthful, making you solid on planet Earth. See the figure 8, the symbol of infinity.

"Feel the love from all directions. See your energy on the third eye screen and adjust it with your brush of light, making your energy incredibly beautiful. See a bubble of light all around your being, a bubble of love and protection that keeps your energy contained and protects you from outside energy."

He then said, "Andrew, I want you to see Yuko on your third eye screen and Yuko, I want you to see Andrew. Look at the energy of the other on the third eye screen and make a note of the colors you see; notice any other intuitive information you can gather from the other. Notice sights, feelings, smells, or sounds that appear. Just notice.

"Now I want you to come out of meditation very slowly and come back to the room."

He asked us how we felt and we both responded that we felt good.

He then asked what I saw when I saw Yuko's energy. I said that I had seen bright purple light radiating above her head, some pink around her back, and white everywhere else. I also said I heard a slight whirring noise and I got a sense of a child's presence around her.

Yuko smiled in acknowledgment and said, "I have a young son."

Mathias asked, "What do the colors mean to you when you try to interpret them?"

I told him that I felt that purple was intuitive energy, white was healing energy, and pink was love.

Yuko then said she saw clear energy around me, with white and red. She said she felt like the white was healing energy radiating from me and that the red was a sort of earthy, focused energy. Mathias then asked each of us to think of someone, we would do some work with, it could be anyone, and then name the person. I mentioned my father and Yuko mentioned her brother.

Mathias then took us through meditation as we connected and surrounded ourselves with light.

He said, "See your third eye screen, and see the person who the other mentioned on the screen. Begin to see their energy. What do you see, what do you feel, what do you smell and hear?

Slowly allow all the information that wants to be revealed to show up on your screen now."

"After assessing their energies, ask the person on your screen if they would be willing to receive healing energy... If they say yes, take your paintbrush of light and brighten up their energy, clearing anything they would like to be healed at this time. Brighten them up if they wish it."

After we came out, we both talked about our experiences. I told Yuko I saw a bit of disconnected energy from her brother's body, some dark spots on his head, which I felt were varied pain and discomfort in his mind, and I felt a somewhat childlike energy around him. Yuko said that made sense because her brother has a mental health condition and wouldn't let the family help him, so he was often homeless. It gave Yuko comfort that he would receive some light, and she felt it would help a bit of the burden that he was carrying during this life.

Yuko then said that she saw that my father had a lot of blue light around him and that he also had an invisible snake that wrapped around his energy. At first, she couldn't interpret the snake, but Mathias looked piercingly at her as if he were pressing her energetically to help her find the words. She then said it was something hidden he kept from others; a sort of addiction that was going to make him sick. I told her she was spot on. She said the blue was a lightness he had, a mental quickness and humor that he exuded. It was a very accurate description of my father.

After this, both Yuko and I were quite amazed at what we had just done. Mathias smiled and talked again about the responsibility of using our energy and the necessity of being respectful.

He then brought up a story. "Once, while leading a meditation group here at my home, a pigeon was sitting on my fence." He pointed through the sliding glass door to a wooden fence. "The beak of the pigeon was hanging as though it had been hurt badly. We went inside and meditated as a group as we had planned. The focus was on healing ourselves, but we also asked the bird if it would like healing. Later, we went outside and found that the bird's beak was positioned properly. Whether one believes that is possible or not is another matter. I highlight this because the potential of this work is unlimited; it's about simply doing it. It can be a great service to ourselves but also to the world as a whole."

We wrapped up the class with Mathias recommending we meditate 30 minutes in the morning and 30 minutes at night.

These new tools gave me a lot to practice, and I would lose myself in meditation at home more and more. The more I meditated, the brighter things became on the inside.

A few weeks later I visited Mathias at The Sage. At this point, he said I should connect personally with Yuko.

I called her and she asked if I had any interest in working with children as a job. I told her I had never considered it before, but I did like kids. She offered me a job and I took her up on the offer and off I went to work as a teacher at a preschool. Since she was one of the board of directors of the school, I was easily hired.

I did not know that I would enjoy working with kids so much. Being creative and making a magical world for them satisfied a deep part of me. On breaks I would meditate, and I felt like I was creating a wonderful and peaceful environment for the children by bringing more peace within myself.

Yuko told me later that she saw through meditation and her intuition that I would be a perfect fit to work with children.

As time went on I found that the work I was doing with Mathias was helping me to see the needs of each child.

Sometimes I would pause and look inside my third eye to see if there was a problem and then assess it from within the right reaction. Meditation helped me be deeply patient and receptive to what these little beings were communicating.

Eventually, the director started placing me with more challenging children since she saw I could work with them. Often, I could see inside my mind that these children were having problems in their home environment, so I was extra patient. I would bring light to the images that appeared in my mind and I tried to be extra loving to a child that was acting out, seeing they were simply expressing some underlying suffering or need.

Occasionally, over the next year, I would consult with Mathias about certain situations. Often, he just listened but on occasion, he would offer a little of his advice, which seemed to come from him working with children who had trauma.

Parents with very challenging children took notice of my way of being and they started asking me if I wanted to watch and care for their children outside of class hours. If I had time, I would take on these extra jobs. My name slowly got passed around to parents for my ability to work with children who had more significant mental and physical challenges. I eventually fully transitioned out of preschool to working directly with children and their families.

During this time Mathias expanded upon his teachings. One afternoon he asked me to meet him at the Arboretum again. We sat on the bench with Luciano and Vincente. He began by explaining that sometimes we are called to certain work at certain times that helps us heal ourselves. If we say yes to the experience in the external world, the challenging part of it becomes a reward in the inner world. He reiterated that this path is one that we traverse alone, and that no one can really do the work for us.

"The idea with this work is not to become reliant on the teacher or the healer to help. Sometimes you need them, but the goal is to make you fully independent within your own vibrational system. Finding the pure radiance and vitality within yourself is the key. Only you can do the work to find that. Healing is not sustainable if others do it for you. When we don't heal on the inside and we consistently rely on those outsides ourselves, the world will start to reflect things we need to face or heal. This can result in a lot of chaos in people's personal lives. Ideally, it's helpful to do the inner work before it slaps us in the face," he laughed.

"Even though this work connects us to all people it is only through our deep individuality that this work shines."

NEAR DEATH, NEAR LIFE

CHAPTER FOUR
THE RAINBOW

Some time had passed when Mathias contacted me for a new lesson. He had me meet him at the park.

Mathias said, "Let's meditate."

The dogs sat between us, and the empty park made for a peaceful backdrop.

He said, "Focus on your breathing, taking deep breaths of light and love and allowing all darkness to flow out, all tension to just disappear into the ether.

"Find your center point and connect to your light systems above and below. Feel deeply connected; be here, be now in this moment. Now I want you to see on your third eye screen what looks like a tunnel forming around us, a tunnel descending from the sky. See it flowing down through the atmosphere and see how we are at the center of this spinning energy, in the eye of a swirling tornado of life.

"And now begin to see a beautiful red color come down this spinning tunnel, a brilliant sparkling red swirling down and then all around us. As it spirals around us, take in this brilliant and beautiful color red. Take in as much as you need. Feel this color and its passion! Feel its aliveness as well as its grounding energy… When you've had enough, just let it go and let the color just swirl around our feet.

"Now let a beautiful, revitalizing orange color come down from above and swirl around us… See how it flows and take in all the vibrancy, absorbing this incredibly creative and life-giving energy. When you have had enough just let it go, allowing it to float around us. Now, see a beautiful yellow come down. This is the color of personified happiness… See it flowing down around us, dancing and spinning. Feel the playfulness and take in all the joyful yellow you need. There is no limit, so just take in what you need or want and let it go.

"Now see a refreshing and revitalizing emerald green come down, spinning around us. Feel it cleanse our breath and clean our world. Take in all you need and then let it go. Now see a light sky blue flowing down and around us, and take in this openness and honest energy. Feel the expansion and freedom to express yourself in the incredible light. Feel how the energy helps express the person you are! Then just let it go and see an indigo, deep ocean blue come spiraling down around us, deepening our experience. Feel its unending wisdom and its strength. Now let it go and see a beautiful purple flow down around us. Absorb as much as you want, this endless and intuitive color, connecting us to new realms and new experiences. Now let it go and see a large and beautiful rainbow swirling around us.

"Now, I want you to watch as all the colors speed up your vibration, swirling faster and faster, turning any density into more and more light. As you allow these lights into your energy field, feel your vibrance increase manifold.

"Now I want you to now see a brilliant white-gold light that shines straight down from the center of this tornado. See it as a pillar of golden light shooting straight into your being, a deeply healing light, and feel it all the way to your bones. Feel the change, feel the transformation. And now let all the colors return to their home, feeling deep gratitude for all the lessons they have brought, all the power they instill, all the love they give. When you are ready, come out of the meditation."

After sitting together for a while, he told me that when sitting at home and practicing these different tools there will be times when visions will come up from the past. In those moments it is good to be present and feel love and connection to oneself, bringing it into the light through simple observation.

He said, "Just witness the scene unfold and breathe in all the past positive energy while breathing out any of the energetic tension, pressure, or darker-colored energy of that time."

Then he said, "Intention is everything."

He told me that if I really wanted to dig into this type of healing, I could make a list of past experiences I felt unresolved about.

He said, "Just see the scenes on your screen appear, breathing in the light of the past and breathing out everything else until the scene lets go and becomes only light."

I told him I understood and that these types of experiences were sometimes happening in my meditations.

He smiled and said, "I think that is enough for today."

CHAPTER FIVE
THE DARK ARTS

It had been a few years since meeting Mathias and my meditation practice had become consistent and deep. I felt my inner world was regularly expanding and, in many ways, it felt like my inner world was more prevalent than my outer world. I was obsessed with these inner energies. Underlying this obsession was a subtle desire to prove something, to reach some overarching goal.

I got a phone call from an old friend from high school. This particular friend was a pretty open fellow with whom I had shared a few meditation experiences. In the middle of the conversation, he said he would be visiting Seattle and he would be with a friend who was also interested in this type of thing. He said she had an interest in meeting me. I thought that was interesting, so a few days later he came over with this young woman.

She was my age and her name was Christine. She was very interested in me and my experience. She asked and asked questions about my training with Mathias. She even asked for specific details and I was glad to share them. It was quite a boost to my ego. The more she asked the more I shared. While

I was talking, I would see her looking into space as if she were thinking to herself deeply. We spent a whole day together talking. She then said she would like to stay for a while longer. I said, "Sure. You can sleep on the couch." As we talked further into the night, she revealed she came from a lineage of healers. I found Christine attractive and after so much conversation and interest between one another, I found myself drawn in to kiss her.

We kissed and as my tongue met her tongue, something felt odd. I recoiled back.

She laughed and then showed me her tongue. It was cut down the middle and looked like a split snake tongue.

After she showed me, I found myself recoiling even more. She smiled strangely as she revealed to me that her mother had cut her tongue during a ritual. She said the ritual was part of their family's tradition. She pushed this uncomfortable feeling deeper as she said that her family dealt in manipulating energy.

After this strange and uncomfortable interaction, I felt very uneasy. Seeing her tongue, all the subtle attraction to her quickly disappeared. I wrapped up our conversation and went to sleep in my room.

I could not sleep all night, which was unusual for me as I was a deep sleeper. Over the course of the night, I developed a stomachache. In the morning Christine said she had slept well on the couch and was headed home.

I told her about my sleep and my stomach. She smiled strangely and said, "I am a healer; let me heal your stomach."

She put her hands on my stomach and I felt an intense, uncomfortable heat come from my stomach. I got super tired and I knew something was very wrong. I wasn't sure what had just happened and I wasn't sure how to process it.

She asked if she could borrow a pair of pants, as she needed some clean clothes to go where she was headed. She said she would return them. I felt that it was definitely a bit odd, but I said sure. I gave her the pants and she left.

After Christine left, I started having bad dreams each night. These slowly became nightmares. Some nights I would dream of a group of people who were trying to do things to me, trying to pin me down and extract something from me. I dreamed of animal sacrifices and strange women trying to lure me in with seduction. I would wake often.

A week or two later I got a call from Christine. She said, "I want to let you know I quit smoking and I used your energy to quit." I knew intuitively that she was trying to get a reaction from me, like a child pushing my buttons. I said okay. Confused and a bit upset, I hung up.

It shook me up, so I meditated. I found my meditation mitigated some of my fear reaction, but I felt off and started to get even more disturbed as time went on.

A week later I heard a knock on my door. I answered it and Christine was standing there unannounced with my pants in hand. She had that similar disturbing smile on her face and said, "I just wanted to return these to you." I thanked her for returning them and explained that I was busy and told her goodbye. I held my pants and looked down at them after shutting the door to find they were covered in dirt. It was like they had been buried, and they had an odd smell. Again, another level of anxiety washed over me with the idea that this psycho lady had done some ritual with my pants. The fear built off and on and I began to feel deeply off balance. At this point, I knew it was time to talk to Mathias.

It was Thursday. I went to The Sage and Mathias was in his usual place, looking again like he was waiting for me. He asked how I was. I said I had had an issue arise and I needed his advice. He didn't say anything, but just listened. I began by telling him that I had met a young woman around my age who seemed to be deeply interested in the energy and spiritual work I was doing. She seemed overly interested and kept asking about all the techniques I had learned. I said that I had told her everything. He interrupted me with a small wave of his hand.

He looked at me and said, "I can't do the work for you; this is the work."

I said I was just wondering what I could do as it appeared there was a group of people working together in some kind of ritualistic way against me. I mentioned how the young lady's mother had trained in the Amazon with healers.

He stopped me and said, "Let's take a clear look at all of this." He asked me to look at myself with my third eye and observe my energy. I had my eyes open and had not done this outside meditation, so I just followed his directions.

He said, "What do you see?"

I said, "I see myself and a strand of energy pushing on me." He nudged me to go on.

"The energy is attached to what looks like a spider web. I see energy being thrown at me in long energy, like strands, particularly toward my stomach where Christine put her hands. I see that they push people off balance with these dark strands of anxiety and fear, pushing on my stomach through anxiety. A type of push and pull."

He said, "Yes, but you are leaving something very important out."

I looked at it and after a moment admitted that I didn't want to admit that I found Christine attractive. I then told him I saw how they knocked people off balance and used seduction through sexual energy to pull the energy toward them, a sort of pull and then a serious push, collecting and controlling people's energy and pulling everything toward themselves.

Mathias said, "Good. So now look at how they have their talons in you. What was it that you did that locked you into this dynamic?"

I said I was trying to prove how special I was and to show how attractive I was to Christine, and that I was trying to show my spiritual specialness, my power.

He said, "Good, that is the lock." He made a hook with his finger. "Now seeing that hook in your third eye, take it out; remove it."

I took it out and then saw a hole. I saw a hole and looked deep into it. He asked what I saw.

I said, "An old wound, a wound of self-acceptance from my childhood."

As I said this, I saw the dark wound transform into myself as a little child. I saw this little me looking for ways to keep my family together before my parents divorced. I saw myself trying to prove to them that I was good enough, searching for acceptance in any way I could. At that moment of realization, I felt a huge relief, as if all this pressure were being released.

Mathias put his hand on my back and told me, "Good work. That is pretty rough. Now see how that wound looks."

I looked to find it had turned to light, and all the presence I was seeing had disappeared. I felt deep compassion for myself at that moment, trying so hard to prove I was worthy of love. I saw I didn't need to prove myself for acceptance from Christine, from women, or from anyone for that matter.

He continued, "Now surround yourself and your home with some brighter light." I visualized a beautiful light of acceptance and love surrounding myself and my home, seeing all the darkness disappear.

I thanked him profusely.

He told me that this was a good lesson in healing. Then he paused and looked out into space. He said, "You know, there are many stories in ancient traditions of dark demon-like energies who come to us as teachers. They come into our lives for a moment using fear and seduction to draw out where we need healing or life lessons. These monsters are simply reflections of inner workings outside ourselves."

I stared at him for a long time, processing what he was saying. I didn't really want to acknowledge that it could be a gift to be preyed on like this.

He looked at me, smiled, and said, "Though... you can always learn in a less dramatic fashion in meditation."

I understood what he meant and smiled back. I could see at that moment that everything negative could be a gift, perceived from one angle.

Mathias then said, "If you look at the day-to-day interactions between people, they aren't always too far off from what you just experienced. Many people are unconscious in their desire for others' attention and energy, for others' blood. Not everyone, but many interactions are not driven by love and by the lightness of joy."

That got me spiraling inside my head. He looked at me and said that was probably enough for today, and so I headed home.

Later I found out through my high school friend who introduced me to Christine that she and her mother were not just part of a small group but were in charge of a cult of many people. He said he had heard through the grapevine that there were maybe hundreds of people who worked with them to do rituals. I told him to be very careful and maybe not spend time with them.

When I meditated and intuitively looked inside myself, I saw so clearly that these people who take from others simply cannot find energy from their own inner Self. Deeply wounded, they feed like animals on the energy of others, like an intense addiction that can't be satiated. It would be so much easier and simpler to connect to their own Source within, but this addiction keeps a cloudy pseudoreality over their eyes.

After this awareness I could only have compassion for those trapped in this cycle of external need. This was such a big recognition that so many people believe their energy and power come from others. Yet, this energy from others is so limited, so small, so insignificant compared to the incredible light and energy that exists within themselves. The energy that extends across the Universe. They simply just need to look for it. Addiction is an addiction in whatever form it appears, and we all have things to work out.

NEAR DEATH, NEAR LIFE

CHAPTER SIX
THE CAVE

I went on with my life and things felt semi-back to normal. A few weeks later I heard a knock on my door. I answered it to find Christine standing staring at me with a weird half-smile on her face. This time I felt no fear when I saw her. She stood there as if hoping for some reaction.

I said, "What can I do for you?"

She looked down, like she was assessing the energy, and as she did this, she appeared to get angry. I could tell she couldn't access my energy.

She stared at me with an eerie look. "It's so easy to control men, they just give it away, they give it all away... It's not my fault they are so stupid. Men are just so stupid."

At that moment I found myself getting very clear and focused, as if a deeper force were taking over me.

I felt myself accessing information from a deep, psychic place and said to her, "It must have been so hard to be forced into this painful cult by your mother. A world where you need to search for energy and take it from others rather than access it from your own Source. It must have been so painful as a little child to be subject to such abuse. I'm so sorry your mother abused you." She looked at me with utter horror and started shaking. Her look of horror shifted, and she burst into tears and then ran away. I felt very proud of myself for helping her see her problems, and I felt vindicated and powerful. I knew I would never see her again.

The feeling of vindication didn't last long. The next time I visited Mathias, I told him what had occurred.

He looked at me seriously and piercingly and said, "Oh! So you tried to heal her without her asking? Why didn't you just shut the door? It sounds like you have some more healing to do around this, no?"

I felt a bit deflated and my ego was saying "But… but… but." So, I went home to do inner work. As I meditated that evening, I clearly saw that part of me that believed I was better than these people who I classified as energetic vampires. I saw how I thought I was more powerful and that I needed to prove that I was. Underlying all of this was a simple word that appeared repeatedly in meditation: "Forgiveness." I couldn't quite embrace the energy of forgiveness and I didn't quite understand at the time how to absorb its energy, so I left it at that.

Over the next few weeks, the word "forgiveness" kept appearing in meditation. I worked on going deeper with it but I just couldn't quite grasp how to embrace it, so I went to visit Mathias. Standing over the ledge, in our usual spot, Mathias said he couldn't answer questions like this for me; this was my own healing to do.

"If I were to do the work for you in this regard then you would just repeat, repeat, repeat." He smiled and said, "Close your eyes. Breathe deep, breathing out all tension and breathing in only light. Now center in your familiar third eye and make your light connections above and below. Now I want you to see yourself sinking a bit, sinking deeper into yourself. I want you to see a cave appear, an earthy, deep cave. I want you now to enter this deep cave within yourself. Sit inside and get a feel for it. I want you to now see your third eye screen appear and I want you to see an experience from your past, any experience, projected on that screen. Just let it appear and begin to breathe in the energy of the past... As you witness the scene, allow yourself to breathe in all the positive energy of that experience, and with each out-breath expel all the heavy weight of that experience. With each in-breath, bring in your past emotions and thoughts, bringing in the brighter part of the past. With each out-breath, intentionally exhale any energy, emotions, and thoughts that are not yours. Feel the light build and begin to see a white flame in the center of the cave. A beautiful white flame. As you begin to let go of the experience on an energetic level, allow any leftover energy to be placed in that flame. Notice that the vision of your past will naturally let go, and imagine breathing it into the fire. Breathe the experience into the white fire. This is a very powerful position for healing and witnessing past experiences."

He said, "There is no limit to how far back you can go in this cave. If the experience is too emotional or overwhelming, just allow it to go back up onto that screen, separating the experience from you. Like watching a movie – seeing the scenes play out, rather than experiencing all the overwhelming emotions and feelings in the movie."

"Now, clear the screen and slowly come out of the cave back to your third eye and back into your body."

Mathias was smiling at me when I opened my eyes, and he asked what I saw. I told him that I saw myself as a little child playing and looking at roly-poly bugs. I saw this as the time period when my parents had been separated. I said that I felt happy, but also felt a little lost emotionally. I sensed a mixture of joy and sadness as I really breathed in the experience. I told him that I felt a burden lifted off the child inside me as I breathed out others' energies that I had attached myself to. I carried expectations and guilt.

"Good," Mathias said. "Now you have a great tool for reviewing your life. The more you practice this, the more space you will clear within yourself. Often people feel lighter and stronger after doing this type of clearing. The potential for transformation is profound."

He added, "This will free your energy up to move into other worlds."

I looked a little shocked at him, wondering what he meant by "other worlds." He didn't say anything more.

I went home and practiced my review. I spent hours reviewing my life and bringing the memories into the light with my breath. The more I delved into it the more I saw how so many parts of my emotional and physical past had influenced my current life. As if peeling an onion, each layer gave me more inspiration to delve deeper. At times certain points of blocked emotional energy were brought up, creating a gateway to seeing yet another deep point in my past. Sometimes these points of energy in time jumped to a later related time, and sometimes they jumped to past experiences that I saw projected on the screen. Sometimes the visions would guide themselves and sometimes I would intentionally guide them.

At one point, sitting in the cave I saw a point of emotional energy in my childhood. This energy buildup was where I hid sadness deep under the face I gave to the world. Underneath the face of happiness was a sadness that I hid behind my smile. As I delved into this childhood sadness it took me into a place of unfolding longing, a deep and wounded longing, a child looking for safety and connection, looking for ways to keep his parents together after their divorce, when I was only four years old. I saw a child clinging to the desire for acceptance from others, acceptance from his parents, acceptance from anyone. No matter which way I turned, I found myself reaching for acceptance in all relationships – it was a locked-in pattern that was visible in my current life. As this awareness came, the scenes in the cave changed and brightened and I felt large layers of heaviness unwinding inside me, as if they were lifting off into space. I saw how that deep search for acceptance got me involved with the dark arts woman. I saw that the desire for acceptance drove me to do things that I wouldn't naturally do. As the light dawned on all of this, a deep healing took place and I felt an intense pressure lift.

* * *

These inner reviews sometimes compelled me to connect with my family members in person. My mother, a very gentle and caring person, was one of them. I knew deep down that I needed to approach her about what I was seeing. I asked her if she noticed that I was unhappy as a child. She said I always seemed very happy and that everything was always great with me. I asked her if there was something underlying this that she wasn't telling me. She said no.

Over the course of a few months I had the same conversation with her and then I asked her why she was very overprotective of me. I told her I felt like she was afraid when I was young. I told her sometimes it felt like this fear superseded the situation. She didn't answer and almost seemed frustrated with my probes.

Some time passed when she came to me and said, "I need to tell you something."

She said that when she was a child her father was not a good man and hurt her and her siblings. She said she never wanted me to have to carry the burden of knowing this, so she never told me. In that moment I could see all the times my mother kept me at bay. In a flash my intuition saw that she didn't want me to become like her father. I could see her deep pain and saw how she wanted to wrap me in protection to keep me safe, but more so keep herself safe. It was a profound moment of opening for both of us. I listened for a long time, absorbing her story, and I thanked her deeply for sharing it with me. I told her I was there for her.

Later, when she told me this story in more detail, I could see a deeper shift occur. The more she shared, the lighter she seemed to become. As if in front of my eyes I could physically see a weight lift from her face as she revealed the trauma. Energetically it looked like a 50-pound weight had been lifted off her shoulders.

After a few months went by, she told me she had decided to confront her father in person. I was a little shocked but deeply supportive.

I saw how this experience was pushing her to confront the familial energy. I said, "I am 100 percent behind you."

Over the next few months, she confronted her parents. They reacted with an outrage that was unbelievable, but my mother stood solid, strong, and stable, like a pillar of truth. Many of her seven brothers and sisters were outraged at her, too. Again, she stood strong and calm as all chaos broke out. Over the course of the next few months a few of her siblings let her know they understood what she had done. She had faced the abuser full force. I was deeply proud of her.

Her healing around this took place on many levels, but the biggest was facing the fact that she was abused and stopped the abuse from happening to anyone else. At one point she was at a store and saw my grandfather. When he saw her, he literally ran away. Soon after, in one of my meditations I saw that if I had not done my inner work in the cave of review, nothing would have changed. The patterns of abuse would have continued, and my grandfather may have abused someone else in the future. I was deeply grateful for the work and how it impacted my family. I felt deeply proud and in awe of the strength of my mother.

The next time I saw Mathias I told him about it. He smiled and said, "That is quite profound, no?"

He then got quiet and looked off in space like he often did and said, "In many traditions around the world there are stories that if you heal yourself, you heal many generations backward, and many generations forward."

He then got an even more serious look on his face and said, "Though you can heal yourself, you can't take responsibility for others' healing; you can only truly heal yourself and be a mirror for others."

He then relaxed and smiled. "You know that you can use the cave of review to go farther back than your childhood, farther than being a baby. How far back is up to you."

This kind of blew my mind open. I had not even contemplated that as a possibility.

As if allowing me to process he paused for a long while and then said, "When doing the life reviews in the cave it is important to not just focus on where you may have been a victim to situations, but it is just as important to see where you have lost energy through your own misuse or abuse of others...

"In the cave of review, it is important to follow the memory threads toward the underlying root cause. Your thoughts are energy and as you ask deeper and harder questions, just allow the memories to resurface on your screen, remembering to breathe in the energy that was lost through those moments of misuse. As you get closer to the root, understanding will slowly dawn. This will potentially bring up very deep emotions, which can be hard to accept sometimes. These emotions and feelings could appear as guilt, shame, self-loathing, and so on. Accepting these feelings with an intention to move deeper will help you unlock even more memories, which in turn will unlock more inner resources. It is important not to force these reviews but to just gently intend."

He paused and looked at me to see if I was following. I lightly nodded.

He continued, "So when you do the cave of review with an intention to clear heavy past stuff like this, it should be done mainly when you feel stable and calm."

"Here are some questions that could be good to ask when you want to dig deeper into the process…

"What energetic words, actions, or thoughts have I used to harm others? Where have I made assumptions about others and where do these assumptions stem from? Where have I wanted to energetically control, possess, or destroy others? Where have I been energetically discriminatory or racist against others? Where have I been unconscious and misused my sexual energy toward others?"

Even though he wasn't asking me to answer him, the weight of Matthias's questions made me feel very heavy. As he spoke each question, many memories flooded my mind.

Noticing my heavy look, he offered some clarification. "I am not saying you are doing these things constantly, but look deeply into your past energetic actions in the cave and you will be surprised to find that you do some or all of these things on a daily basis, unconsciously of course. Everyone carries these energies. Seeing them, feeling them, and then transforming them will begin an energetic resolution where you can then transform and repair yourself and your past, present, and future relationships...

"The more you take responsibility for your energetic actions without a judgment of 'bad' or 'good' the more you will take responsibility for your reality and the more freedom you will incur."

I went home and over many months dug deeply into the cave, seeing situation after situation appear where I was unconsciously biased, where I was unconsciously judgmental, where I was unconsciously wanting to control situations – each time breathing in the past energy and putting all the leftovers in the white flame, seeing it transform. I would so often lose track of time during this process, spending hours reviewing, always looking to place the next piece into the light and to get to that deeper reasoning, that deeper understanding.

CHAPTER SEVEN
THE ELEMENTS

Mathias said we should meet at his home, as there were some more tools he wanted to share with me. I met him there, at the familiar lower level of his house, where I was welcomed by my two friends Luciano and Vincente.

He said, "Today we are going to take a little step deeper into your work."

He asked me to get comfortable as we would be meditating for a while.

He said, "Now, take some deep breaths, sinking deeper within yourself and allowing all the tension to release out of you. Breathe in light and love, knowing you can simply center yourself inside and connect to your inner Source at any time, in any situation in life. Your Source is always there with you. Keep breathing... Now feel a deep love for your Source and send that light and love above you to the Universe and allow it to return to you in brilliant white light. Then send it down into the earth and feel yourself become deeply stable and grounded with golden light from below, from the magnetic center of the earth.

"Now, centering back in the center of your mind, see a path opening up for you. As this path expands, follow it. Follow that path to a deeper point inside you, into a clearing…

"As you enter this clearing, I want you to see and feel the energy of the element of earth appear before you. Just allow the element of earth to approach you. See where the element of earth takes you – maybe it brings you to a forest of trees or maybe some deep clay, dirt, or stone. Wherever it takes you, allow the energy of the earth to begin to speak to you. Feel its presence, see its colors, smell its scents, listen to its message to you.

"After receiving its message, slowly begin to see yourself merging with it, becoming one with the earth, letting go of tension into the deep, nurturing energy. Now see the earth that surrounds you slowly turn to light, a beautiful, earthy light shining brighter and brighter. Pure, brilliant, earthy energy. Feel this light and absorb this light into yourself. Become one with it. See how it helps you; see how it functions and feels. Know you can connect with this light and the element of earth at any time.

"Now slowly come out of that space and return to your path. Notice on this path that a form of water appears, maybe a stream or a lake, or maybe rain… Just allow water to come to you and be with you. Listen to its sounds, smell the smells, and notice any tastes. Then begin to let go and become one with the water. Feel it flow, feel it dissolve into you and move you. Feel its dance and in its peace. Slowly see this water become light. Feel it getting brighter and brighter, and feel this light merge with you, healing you, going to where you need it inside you. Communicate with it… feel it… Now let it go and then come back to your path."

He proceeded, "As you continue, I want you to begin to see a fire in the distance, and I want you to get closer to the fire. Seeing its beauty… its warmth… its healing heat. Listen to its message and its wisdom. What does it smell like? What does it feel like?

Allow yourself to gently merge with the dancing fire, letting go of your pains, letting it energetically burn away all your fears. Now, stepping out of the fire see it turn into a brilliant, joyful light, and slowly merge with the light of fire. Feel it become one with you and see how it can be used in meditation for healing.

"Let it go now and return to your path. I want you to begin to feel a wind blowing. This could be a desert wind or an ocean wind. Begin to feel it. See the wind blowing over the other elements; listen to its sound. Feel the air, like the breath of all life. Feel yourself become one with the air, flowing through the tree leaves, dancing over hills, breathing over the mountains. Feel the wind carry away anything heavy... Now slowly see it turn into a beautiful light. Notice the color of this light, individual to you. Notice its brilliance and merge with the light of the wind and know it is you.

"Anytime you want to come here and merge with these elements, you can. I want you to return to the path now and I want you to see all four elements dancing around you. See them as they spiral in light. Watch as the brilliant colors of all the energies on this planet dance through and with you. Feel yourself be one with them. At any time, you can come back here, honoring them, listening to them, and working with these magical elements. They are you and you are them. As time passes you may find they are doorways to other worlds...

"Slowly start walking back down that path toward yourself, and end up at your third eye. Begin to slowly feel your body and when you are ready, come out of meditation." Mathias was smiling at me when I opened my eyes.

He asked how that had gone for me. I responded, "I feel like a new person. I moved through a beautiful forest, smelling the bark, feeling the tree branches, and then flowed into the deep soil beneath it. I touched the colors and felt the power of trees and the earth as my very own self.

"Then I felt oneness with an ever-expansive ocean, seeing sea life and coral, swimming in colors that I didn't know existed. I felt those colors as part of myself. I saw fire and flame consume my being and then I traveled within the earth with flaming layers of lava and stone. I felt one with a desert wind blowing over an orange-sanded desert, making shapes in the sand. I danced as the desert air, in gentle harmony and perfection with all the air between the earth and space. I could smell the sand in the wind, the fire in the air. It was incredible."

Mathias said, "As you just experienced, the potential for travel and healing with these elements is deeply profound. As you practice and connect, you can see what wonders will take place."

He looked serious for a moment, "In the past, many cultures knew how to connect to these elements and in some cases, they misused this energy. The idea is to connect, relax, and deeply listen to them, respecting them. This is freedom. To control nature and try to harm her will often result in a personal prison. This is a subtle awareness that is valuable not just in meditation but in all areas of life. Respect for the elements is a reflection of respecting all life and of respecting yourself."

I went home and returned to my life. I found the elemental work deeply powerful. I worked with multiple elements, and sometimes just one at a time. Slowly it started to dawn on me that everything in the world on the outside was on the inside. I could feel myself beginning to dance with beautiful energies, communicating with their wisdom and energy. There was great freedom in knowing that I could simply close my eyes and be in a beautiful scene. When I wasn't meditating, I felt more and more connected to plants and trees, the air I breathed, and the entire earth. I had a new respect for the aliveness in nature. There was so much to embrace and learn from these energies.

CHAPTER EIGHT
WHITE TIGER, RED HAWK

Some time had passed since I had had a class with Mathias, and my meditations had become more involved. I sometimes worked with elements, sometimes the rainbow, and sometimes the cave. I always connected to the Universe above and the earth below. At one point I was doing my normal meditation and suddenly I felt a slight pull inside me. It was as if something was tugging to my left. I felt a presence and then saw stripes appear against a background as if something were walking in front of my third eye.

This occurrence started to happen more and more until one day I saw a full outline of a white tiger come into my meditation. This became a daily occurrence. At first, it would frustrate me as I wanted to focus on my other practices. As I started to surrender to the fact that the tiger was not leaving, I slowly began to let it guide my meditations. It started taking me on journeys into the elements, walking into nature scenes within myself.

As these started to get more in-depth, the journeys started expanding into beautiful new energies within myself. Each time the journey would go a little deeper.

There was a fierceness, yet deep love I felt while working with the tiger, and at some point we merged, as one. I was so enamored with the inner tiger that I bought a large carpet with a form of a tiger on it. I could lightly sense how this white tiger helped me work with children. It helped me to feel the energy of presence, motherly care, creativity, and deep nurturing strength and groundedness.

The next time I visited Mathias at The Sage I mentioned the tiger. He stayed quiet for a long time, returning to his usual piercing stare. As we sat in silence for a while, I wondered what he was assessing.

He said that this was a natural progression of this work. He said it was a good time for me to meet a sister colleague of his. I was a little shocked to hear he had a colleague like himself; I had not considered that I would ever encounter more people like Mathias.

He said, "She is a teacher like myself but with her own gifts. Her name is Okami and she will be able to work with you in the power of healing. I will set up a time for you to meet her."

I went to an address provided by Mathias. It was about 30 minutes north of Seattle. I found the home and knocked on the door. When it opened an extremely large white wolf with blue eyes was standing there, staring at me. There was a woman holding its collar, but I hardly noticed her as the wolf was motionless and staring into my eyes.

The woman said, "This is Vala. She is a wolf."

I was a bit shocked and stunned by this introduction. As I relaxed and realized I wasn't going to be eaten, I reached my hand out to pet the wolf. The woman said that wolves didn't have a sense of humor, so being playful wasn't a great idea. She seemed to read my thoughts, because my next move would have been to be more playful. As I looked into Vala's eyes I could see the wild animal still in her and so I treaded carefully as I went into the home.

As I stepped into the Spanish-style home, I noticed art from all over the world, beautiful and striking paintings with deep golds and many rich colors that lined the walls. The woman greeted me and said her name was Okami. She had a warm but very direct presence and there was a bit of wildness about her energy. Her hair was all white like Mathias's, and I couldn't help noticing how similar it was to the color of the wolf.

She had me relax and make myself at home. After she showed me around, we went downstairs to a very large room. The place smelled of incense and there was a small fountain near the middle of the room. I wasn't sure what to expect, so I felt a little anxious. Wasting no time, we sat down, and she immediately started teaching. She said that the path that I had been traversing with Mathias was a path that really put a person on the spot, making one walk the line of responsibility.

She looked at me with a calm, expressionless focus. "Do you understand what I mean when I say responsibility?"

I said I felt she meant that I don't project my energy and my life onto others, that in a way responsibility was a sort of deep inner silence. She nodded and smiled.

She then went on, "Today we are going to begin the process of some deeper healing, eventually leading to you being able to work on others. With this work comes a deep responsibility. Within yourself, you will need to be strong like a warrior, the universal warrior who stands with integrity and unwavering like the sunrise.

"You will need to stand lovingly and remain compassionate like the universal healer who stands nurturing, like the moon over the ocean."

She went on, "You will need to stand tall and stable like the universal teacher, an immovable tree of wisdom flowering in many different directions. You will need to stand present like a leader, the universal leader who leads like a mountain, unwavering, and supportive in your love for everyone. One who leads by example not by control. How these will manifest will be individual to you.

Now let us meditate."

She told me to sit back and deeply relax. "Allow all the tension to flow out and start to take slow, deep breaths, breathing in deeper and deeper with each in-breath, sinking into the center of yourself."

She continued, "Now allow yourself to sink down, shifting deeper and deeper below as if sinking into the deepest part of the earth within you. Begin to see a light, like a light at the end of the tunnel... As you approach this light, see a beautiful scene appear. This is a place of sacredness and power. Stand at this doorway and just breathe in this new experience deeply connected to the earth, deeply connected to your inner light. As you walk into this scene, begin to see all the beautiful elements that appear before you – the earth below, the wind blowing, the waters flowing, and the clouds above.

"Now as you enter this beautiful plane or power, begin to feel a presence approaching you, walking toward you from the East. This is the essence of the East, the pure energy of the East, your inner warrior. See this warrior come and meet you. See how beautiful and strong they are, like all the colors of the sunrise. Notice their appearance, their face, their gender, and ask them if they have a message for you. Receive the message gifted to you at this moment... Now begin to see this warrior turn brighter and brighter until they become a brilliant, pure light that is shining. No form; only light. Now merge with the light, taking what you need as you see yourself as one with the light of the East, and know you are the brilliance of the East.

"Now let that energy go and turn in the opposite direction to see a new, deeply peaceful and calming presence approach you. This is the healer of the West. A deep and luminous presence like the colors of the moon and ocean. See them approach and see what they look like. Greet the healer of the West, and ask if they have a message for you. Slowly watch them turn into an incredible shining light. Allow yourself to become one with this light, the light of the West. See this light as simply as your very own Self.

"Now turning to your right, feel the fearless and loving leader of the South approach. Feel their powerful and caring presence. What do they look like to you? Are they female or male or both? Ask them if they have a message for you. Receive the South's message. Now see them slowly turn into an incredible light, the light of the South, and merge with that light, becoming entirely one with South. Know this is your very own Self. Then as you let the South go, feel its strength remain.

"Now see the teacher of the North approach you, a divine and endlessly wise teacher who comes in a particular form. Let the teacher speak to you, giving you a message that you need to hear. See the teacher turn into the brilliant light of the North. Merge with the North's wisdom and direction. Breathe in this new, brilliant wisdom and recognize it as your very own Self.

"Now see all four directions in the form of light, standing firm and strong on each side of you. See the collective light of the warrior, the healer, the leader, and the teacher! Feel the radiance and luminescent light of the four directions and know at any time you can come to meditate here and be with these beings of light. See how these energies can guide and protect you, and know these beings are as one with your very own Self."

After a moment of quiet Okami said, "They have always existed inside you, as well as outside – they are you. Now ever so slowly come out of the journey, coming slowly back into your body and into the moment."

As I came out of this experience, I felt immensely different and strong, like an inner power had taken hold. I felt an infusion of new energetic information.

Okami said she would like to meet with me three more times to develop and stabilize my energy into the role of the healer.

She concluded our meeting with an insight: "This work is universal and ideally it can translate across cultures. In the end, it is all light and an expression of our own Self, given at the right time."

* * *

I went home to practice what I had learned.

* * *

I met Okami at her home again for our second meeting. This time as she walked me downstairs, she began telling me that to hold space for others was one of the gifts of this work we were doing. "The more one meditates, the more one can hold a space of presence for others, ideally getting to a point of clear walking meditation. This expands and results in answering the momentary call where Spirit wants us to be guided through surrender to each moment. This is ideal, of course."

She continued, "One way to be aware is to see yourself walking between two worlds."

She looked at me for a moment and asked if I understood what she meant by walking between two worlds. I told her I felt it meant that I could see the worlds inside myself but still be completely grounded and present. She smiled and nodded. "To be in the world, but not of it, holding light and space."

She went on to say, "In many traditions around the world animals are a big part of spiritual healing, particularly Earth-based cultures. The journey and the resonance with certain animals reflect certain energies that can benefit or give lessons. Some people resonate with the energy of animals and some don't. Today, we are going to journey within ourselves to meet guides in animal forms."

She paused and looked at me and said, "It sounds like you have already been doing this." I wasn't sure if she knew because Mathias told her, or if she just knew.

She said, "Let's meditate. Close your eyes, breathing in light and love, letting out all tension, all pressure. Just let it all drop away. Now, center yourself within your being and allow yourself to just sink deep, deeper, and deeper, traveling deep into the earth within you. Allow yourself to keep flowing deeper until you reach a beautiful plane of existence, a plane of power deep within the earth, deep within you. See the stunning nature of this beautiful place, this familiar place. Now walk out into this natural area and call out to a guide in animal form. Call out and state that you would like to meet a guide in animal form. See the animal approach; see its power, its strength. Whatever the animal is, let it come to you and communicate with you. Interact with this animal and see what lessons it brings with it."

After some time, she said, "Slowly begin to see the animal brighten into a beautiful light of varied colors and merge with this light, feeling yourself and it as one. Feel the power of connecting with this guide. Now separating, allow yourself to let the animal go, thanking it for the honor of its presence and its guidance. Now let yourself come back from your journey and come back toward your body. Up, up, up until you are fully back in your body." She was smiling when I opened my eyes.

She asked how that had gone for me. I responded, "More than one animal came. First, a tiger and then a hawk. I merged with each animal separately, flying over rivers and valleys as a hawk. I felt an extreme focus, freedom, and expansion as I spread my wings, floating above it all. I felt as if I was one with the sky, with a piercing focus. When I merged with the tiger I felt strength, love, and deep nurturing. I felt I could hug the entire world with my presence, ground things with my paws, all the while being fully active and passionate."

She said, "Great! Now practice, practice, practice, and come back in a month."

As I practiced at home connecting with my guides, their reasons for appearing started to become clearer and clearer. The hawk is an independent creature, flies alone, and goes its own way. It follows its own trajectory while maintaining a high vision. Hawks are independent and unmoved by smaller birds, by the things below.

My apartment had a small deck with a view of the Space Needle. I would often sit in my orange velour chair and meditate. One cool morning, sitting peacefully and journeying with the hawk inside myself, I opened my eyes to see a real-life hawk sitting not too far away from my deck on a tree. It was staring right at me. I could see every detail, the reddish color and its striped tail, and the energy exuding from it was peaceful, precise, and powerful. I closed my eyes for a moment and connected with my inner hawk, feeling that same energy, feeling deeply grateful inside and out for the experience with a deep recognition that the natural world was guiding me. When I opened my eyes, the hawk was gone.

New animals would sometimes appear, sharing lessons, light, and energies, and then familiar ones would disappear. On another day I had a dragonfly come into my meditation. As I opened my eyes, a few feet from my face was a dragonfly gliding around. As Mathias always reminded me, the little or big experiences on the outside are just reflections of the inside, but it's hard not to be in awe at the magic of the Universe when such alignments happen.

* * *

I was delving deeper into myself than I had before and I could see how all the elements and beings of nature are within us, in different forms. I found myself more interested in the inner world than the outer. In a way, I started to judge the outside world and considered it less important than the inner. I found a new ego developing around this and a desire to not really want to be in my day-to-day life. My job was still meaningful, but it paled in comparison to meditating.

During this time, I was no longer working independently with children and families. A parent had recommended me to be an assistant to a psychologist that ran a holistic therapy center for children with mental and physical challenges. This therapy focused on sensory-motor integration and auditory processing. Most of the children who came into the office were diagnosed on the autism spectrum, while some had behavioral or mental health challenges. I would take care of the children, helping maintain their therapy and I would make sure that they were receiving their treatment without disturbance to themselves or the other children.

Over time I noticed how my meditations helped me stay calm and present for these children. In the back of my mind, I had always hoped that the extra light I brought into my meditations would also add to the therapy that the children were receiving. On rare occasions I would have the thought that maybe I was the one helping the kids… Until one day, a young girl I had been working with walked up to me and said, "Andy! I had a dream about you! I was stuck under a huge rock.

I couldn't move and I was in so much danger, but you came along and lifted that rock up and I was able to get free!"

I told her that was a great dream. Inside my head, I associated it with the work that I did in meditation and I was very proud of myself.

The next day the same girl came in and said, "Andy! I had another dream about you! You were stuck under a huge rock, in a lot of danger, and I came and lifted that huge rock and you were set free!" At that moment I got a very powerful and ego-busting lesson.

When you help someone, you are helping yourself, and when you help yourself in a positive way, you are helping others. I had realized before what a gift it was working with children, but this experience deepened that realization, as I saw that the gift of working with these children was more for my healing than theirs. These children were a great gift, as they helped me integrate many parts of myself, helped me develop patience and love, and helped me form deeper understandings about myself that I never would have realized without the gift of working with them.

CHAPTER NINE
LAPIS LAZULI

The next time I met with Okami she said it was time to talk about past lives. "Some people may not believe in past lives and that is totally okay. Everyone's belief systems are valid. What we are seeing when we see past lives can be equally diverse depending on individual views, yet it can still be universal. For some, it can simply represent unconscious images, archetypes, or psychic impressions of things that need healing within themselves.

"Believing in past lives or not, the work is the same. The images are being given to you as a representation of something needing healing. These energies come from deep within yourself to help you see your hidden pain and problems."

She continued, "When you are shown a past life, it is best to not be concerned with that life and the experiences of that time period. The idea is to find the root of the problem and pain that is blocked up in your personal energy. The goal is to get to the reason that this particular life, this archetype, is being shown to you. There is a pattern that has been passed into your present life that can be released. Finding the root and pattern can then help a person unhook and then heal an issue that is affecting them in the present day. It simply takes an intention to clear the pattern and pain completely off the energetic field."

She paused to let it sink in and then said, "Some people see life intuitively, as symbols. When meditation is practiced, the energy of these symbols becomes fluid energy, a fluid constant. As these symbols becomes more available to the individual who psychically sees, one's experience expands. Slowly everything in a person's day-to-day life becomes a symbolic message, not just internally but externally as well. There is a beautiful opening that happens when one can dance through life, flowing with universal archetypes, universal symbols. One's life becomes a walking message." She paused again. "But this is for a later teaching."

She then prepared me for meditation. First, she guided me into my connections. "I want you to allow yourself to sink deep, deep into the plane of power. When you are there, I want you to connect with your inner animals, seeing their light merge with your light. Now I want you to begin to see a new cave on this plane. A cave that has a deep blue color. I want you to approach this beautiful blue cave. A blue color lines the walls of the cave, the color of lapis lazuli. A deep, rich blue. This is the cave of past-life review."

She said, "As you enter and then sit in this cave, see a deep blue flame of transformation burning in the center. This flame is also the color of lapis lazuli or possibly a blue sapphire. This is the flame of transformation. You will use this flame to clear patterns from your past lives.

"See this flame build deeper and brighter, letting it transform any part of yourself that needs clearing in this moment.

"Now, see a pool of water in the cave. Walk over and peer into this reflective pool of water. Slowly allow a past life to appear in this pool. This is a special place where you can go deeper into healing in the subtle and dream-body consciousness."

As she said this, I saw a past life appear in the reflection. It was an ancient Roman time period and I could see and feel chains on my ankles.

She said, "As you see this life appear, look to the emotional energies locked up in the time period. Notice the area in your physical body where this pain is stuck."

At first, it was hard to make out the energy. Then like a movie I saw how my life played out in Rome. I could feel myself restrained in chains, subjugated to work for others, forced into submission. In that time period, I had a strong will, and the more I was oppressed the more resentful I felt of authority. I saw how the authority of the time used me in entertainment because of my strength. I could smell the dust on the ground and could see the blood on my ankles where the chains had been placed for so long. I felt the pain in my physical body.

She then said, "See how these emotions get locked in at the time of death."

I saw myself die as a form entertainment for others, stabbed through the side with a metal spear, feeling worthless and a victim of the world.

She then said, "Use the lapis lazuli flame to clear the pain off your physical body. Lift it off. See the emotional hook and go deeper with it. See how it unwinds and lifts off, and with each layer revealed you can sink deeper into the issue. Now, place these heavy energies into the lapis lazuli flame. See the energies transform into a sparkling light that dissipates into the ether."

She said, "When doing this type of clearing the idea is to unlock the pattern at the very root, seeing calmly the emotional, intellectual, and physical issue, and then let it all burn away.

Imagine clearing the dross so you don't have to carry it in today's world."

I spent some time really looking at this life. She then asked if there was anything left from that life still lingering in the pool of reflection. I saw a piece of grief, so I went deeper into it. I saw how I longed to protect my wife and child who I had been ripped away from. We lived in a small village near the sea and after being forcibly taken I felt deeply helpless. I couldn't be there with them, to protect them, to provide for them, and to love them. This left deep energy points of pain inside my subtle being that traveled with my spirit after death. The feeling of guilt, of not knowing, of not being good enough, and of not being able to provide ate deeply at my heart and mind.

As I began clearing and lifting this energy, I then saw patterns that connected to my current life, especially in my unhealthy need to care for others. This underlying energy from a previous life existed as a deep, subtle guilt around abandoning others. I saw how I worried in this life that others might think I would abandon them. Seeing my present guilt and worry from this new perspective helped me lift out the energy even more and clear it. Layer after layer of energy had made its way to my present life from my past. I placed it all into the blue flame. I did this until I no longer saw any past life. All I could see was a beautiful deep blue light.

Then, as if sensing I had completed my work, Okami had me come out of meditation. She said, "When clearing we should always be positioned in the lapis lazuli, the deep blue cave within us."

She asked me what that experience was like. I told her I had felt a lot of deep, intense emotions. I saw how I carried issues over to this life and I felt them completely lift and shift when focusing on the flame. After I placed these issues fully in the flame, I could no longer feel the energy of the past life or see it on the screen, almost as if it had disappeared. I thanked her deeply for this newfound experience.

Okami said, "It's important to remember that you have been given these tools to truly do your own healing. Healing can be done on someone else, but if the inner work is not done within yourself then you won't be able to help others as in-depth. Healers who don't do their own inner work produce little depth and often create codependence between the themselves and the people they are healing.

"When it comes to the flame, you cannot see the depths of others if you cannot see your own deep blue depths… Look to places in nature with deep blues, the depth of their presence, the depth of their wisdom, and notice how you feel when you stare into their depths. Whether it be the sky or the ocean, there is an eternal expansiveness. Know you are the lapis lazuli; you are one with the blue light of healing."

She smiled for a moment and said, "Not doing your own work is like going on a diet but waiting impatiently for the end of the diet to eat some rich and greasy pizza. The idea is for long-lasting, sustainable change – not a short-term pat on the back."

She continued, "If you do decide to start doing hands-on healing with others, then it is an agreement between you and the person. It is an acknowledgment that one person is expressing the energy for the other who might not be able to see the issue. It is important to note that only when the person receiving is willing to acknowledge the trauma energetically can it be released. If you force, then no clearing can take place. Only in letting go can the transformation truly take place."

She then guided me to lie on the floor. She held my feet for a moment. She said she would now show me some hands-on work.

Almost in sync with us moving to the floor Okami's wolf, Vala, came over and started sniffing me. Okami said Vala was sensing the healing that was about to take place. She said that animals were often sensitive to this type of work. Vala seemed to hover over me and sniff the air above me, and then she lay down next to me. As she lay down, I could feel her strong presence as if she were holding me stable, grounding me.

Okami told me to focus on my connection to the earth as she let go of my feet. She moved to the side opposite Vala and put her hands slightly above my feet. She told me she was about to start clearing energy with the lapis lazuli flame and that all I needed to do was relax and listen. It would be up to me to let the energy go if I wanted to release it. She began doing a reading of my past lives, first relaying a life where she saw me as a young man running from attackers in ancient Europe. In this life I tripped and ended up twisting my ankle, which is why she felt the energy in my foot. Deep fear was locked in as the attackers overtook me. She saw it hooked into my energy emotionally as a pattern of always feeling like I must run away. She said she also saw a fear of being unstable and being out of control with life. She said it got locked into this area at my death when the attackers killed me. She cleared off the helplessness, the fear of being out of control.

She then said, "The emotions you feel today related to committing solidly to yourself are a translation of the pain of that life."

She then told me she was going to place that life in the blue flame. She cupped her hands above my energy and then blew into them. I felt an immediate release, and everything she was seeing and saying became clear and made perfect sense to me. She did three more lives like this, moving up my body and clearing my energy field. She finished by waving her hands across my body and told me she was visualizing spreading the flame across my energy field, clearing any residual negative energies.

After this work was done, she had me lie quietly for a long time, and I fell asleep. When I woke, she gave me some water and told me to work inside with my lapis lazuli cave and then come back in a few weeks.

When I got home, I found myself feeling so healthy, as though my energy had been opened up to fresh air. I felt clear, and yet a bit overwhelmed psychologically by this process. I could not fully comprehend the healing that had just taken place. Though it seemed beyond my ability I persevered and went into the lapis lazuli cave within myself often. I would allow lives to come and be cleared. I found the deep blue cave much different and much deeper than the white flame in the life-review cave where Mathias had brought me many years ago. I used the white flame review often to reclaim my energy, but the blue flame added a layer that felt way beyond my connections to this life. I let myself delve deep into this work, but part of me intuitively knew that there was a fine line between witnessing past lives and getting absorbed or obsessed with the experiences that I was being shown. Keeping an emotional and intellectual distance was important in order to maintain perspective.

On the next visit Okami took me into the blue flame cave again in meditation. This time she had me go to my pool of reflection.

She said, "Now going a little deeper, I want you to see one of your very first lives on planet Earth. If you can, I want you to go all the way back and see what you see when you let yourself first appear on Earth as a human."

At first, all I could see was a red light. A deep, earthy red light… and then slowly a life appeared. A very simple life, where I was part of a community that lived outside, in a reddish desert area. I felt a deep connection to nature and the earth. I could see an incredible night sky that would appear every night filled with endless stars. I felt I was in the womb of the comforting earth. I could clearly feel the energy, and it felt powerful to be connected to this deep-rooted memory.

Okami had me slowly come out of the meditation and said, "Traveling along these lines, you could go even deeper and explore beyond your first life as a human."

She gave a mischievous smirk that I often saw on Mathias's face. "It's simply about doing the work."

Before I left, she said she would like to introduce to me another colleague of hers. She said that this colleague had a special gift of working with the body and energy. She said her name was Joon and she had studied martial arts all over the world, from South Korea to Japan and China. She had a lifetime of practicing with masters in Qi Gong, Kung Fu, Tai Chi, Yoga, and more. I said I would be very interested, so she said she would connect me.

Joon was to meet me at Okami's home on a specific day. When that day came, Okami sent me downstairs but didn't come with me. I found a woman seated there, with straight black hair and a very strong presence. Her facial expressions were serious. Though she was not large, her energy made me feel very small. She introduced herself and said it was nice to meet me.

I said I was excited to learn something new and told her Okami had shared with me that she was a martial artist.

She nodded and then said that she had come to share with me some work involving breath and healing the body. "It is not unusual in the work you have been doing that you start to have daytime flashes of past lives and how to perform certain acts from those past lives."

She asked, "Do you sometimes have memories of being a monk?" It kind of shocked me because I wasn't expecting those words, but I thought back for a moment and I acknowledged to her that I did have a familiarity with certain monks.

Her look became more focused and she said, "Do you remember when you practiced martial arts as a monk?" Her intense eyes were looking right through me and it was as if her words brought back a slew of ancient memories of me in a red robe, near a mountain, doing particular moves. I was a warrior monk, and I could feel and see the movements as I practiced. I could even see deadly moves that I practiced regularly. I could recall some of them and attempted to move my body, imitating some of the moves. She laughed a bit and said that might be something I would want to meditate on. I remembered in that moment that I shouldn't get obsessed with past lives, but it would be very interesting to get skills from other lives if possible.

Joon said, "Okami said she would like me to teach you a simple but deeply profound practice I have learned over time." She had me lie on the ground. She said she wanted me to breathe normally.

"Notice your breathing… Now, deepen your breath… and begin to breathe deeper into your belly." She paused while I breathed more deeply.

Then she continued, "Breathe even deeper, into the lowest part of your belly. Feel the breath build and become more and more buoyant. See the breath become light in your deepest belly. Now feel it go even deeper beyond and move your breath completely into your energy field below you. Feel and experience the energy field that is below your feet, and feel each breath brighten that field until you feel a natural pull that brings that breath into your feet, feeling the light breathing in your feet."

"Now breathe into your feet, feeling as if your feet are breathing in and out, each breath brightening your feet while it expels any stagnation, any stuck energy. Now slowly breathe this into your hands, feeling the light breath. Every breath can be a healing moment.

"Then breathe into your head, lighting up your head, and now breathe into your chest and torso, and now back into your belly."

She continued, "When we are babies we breathe deeply into our bellies and the life energy moves easily through us in waves of laughter or crying. The light is normal for babies, but as we get older or sick we begin to breathe higher and higher in the chest until we are barely breathing. This high, shallow breathing is an indicator of loss of life, loss of physical body light. The power of conscious light breathing can transform you into a more youthful being."

She then told me to stand up, and she showed me a couple of physical movements that brought energy from all around me and into my belly.

After she finished, she told me that Okami had asked her if I could do past-life clearing work with her and she had agreed. I could tell that I would learn a lot from working from Joon; her worldly wisdom and knowledge seemed deep, and her experience of body-healing modalities would help me learn and grow. I looked forward to the healing sessions.

* * *

The next time I met with Okami, Joon was there.

Okami said, "We are going to do a meditation, and then Andrew will practice healing work on Joon."

She centered us and had us activate our inner connections, and then to the four directions. When we came out, she said to me, "Each time you meet with Mathias or me, the energy builds upon the last lesson. You should always strengthen the past energies to build on the future. I would like you each to do a clearing of three lives on each other."

She had Joon lie down and continued, "First you will want to make sure Joon is grounded to the earth. Gently hold her feet and imagine a deep, grounding, and beautiful light coming up through you from the center of the earth then into her feet, holding her steady. This will be both deeply grounding for you and for her. Feel the light stabilize both of you, holding yourself as one with the earth."

She had me place my hands slightly above Joon's head and told me to feel light from the Universe coming down into her being. "It is not about forcing or even doing something. It is about gently intending."

I recognized the similarity to what Mathias had said, and I understood what she was saying. As I sat above Joon with my hands about six inches away from her head, I focused on bringing light through me.

Okami then said, "Now go to Joon's feet and place your hands a little above them. You should always start the clearing in the lower energy centers and slowly move up to the head, toward the higher energy centers. You can do the clearing in any fashion, but ideally, it is good to do it in three life clearings or seven life clearings, along the major energy centers of the body. Today we will do three." She continued, "Stay centered, keeping your hands steady, slightly above the body, and begin to start intuitively reading the energy."

I felt a little shaky, and there was intense heat in my body. Okami said that it was normal to feel intense heat or cold when doing this work. She said my energy was adjusting to being in a new position. I felt instantaneously a twinge of something in my hands. I said that I was seeing and feeling life. Okami told me to say it out loud for Joon to hear.

I said out loud that I saw a very poor person in Thailand, and that she had to beg for everything in her life. Though this individual was of positive disposition she got deeply sick. This illness down-spiraled the already challenged existence and she became deformed and could not walk.

Okami said, "Find the emotional hook."

I said, "It is a feeling of deep helplessness and a constant state of loss of control."

Okami, "Now find the pattern and lock."

I said, "The pattern that got locked in was the fear of being helpless to circumstance. so Joon in this life tries to control circumstances."

As I made this connection, I felt some energy shift.

Okami then asked me to find her death, where the final lock would be.

I saw suffering in Joon's past life and a great relief when she died. I felt her subtle energy did not want to be in human form again after all that suffering. I told Joon I saw a deep, underlying control over her own energy. This deep control manifested as desire to be entirely with Spirit, rather than human. This drove Joon to be extremely disciplined in spiritual matters and kept her away from many connections to people in the world.

After telling her all that I saw, I felt an energetic shift, a sort of letting go. I then lifted the heavy energy out and blew it into the deep blue flame of transformation in front of me.

Okami was staring intently at what we were doing, appearing to look deeply at something on a subtle level. She smiled and said, "Good work." I saw Joon's face appear more relaxed after I blew the problem into the blue flame. Joon remained silent as I continued.

I cleared two more lives in a similar fashion. Near the end, Okami had me scan the rest of Joon's energy for any leftover issues, and then swoop my hands over the energy field seeing any leftover negative energy go into the lapis lazuli flame. She had me hold Joon's feet and run a grounding light through them until Joon was ready to get up.

Okami said that this work was very deep, and it could take a while for people to feel ready to come back to the world. She said for some it could be very emotional. She also said that at any point when doing this work if I felt stuck I could call in the light of my animal guides or the elements to help guide my work.

Okami said that this concluded the healing training for now. She told me she would like me to practice with Joon as much as possible, focusing on clearing past lives. She said this work was most powerful when done on oneself, and that was the most important thing. Doing my own work was most important. Okami said that working with someone experienced like Joon would help my energy speed up, refine, and strengthen for work I would be doing in the future.

I was excited to practice more and more. Joon and I set up a time to meet weekly. We would meet at one of our homes and do clearing sessions.

Joon's home was south of Seattle. Beyond being a martial artist, she was also a sculptor and multimodal artist. She created lifelike sculptures and art from things she saw in her meditations and dreams. She used natural substances she found in nature. Her home felt a bit like entering another world with beings made of natural art, sticks, clay, and stone.

Joon shared with me that many years ago she had come down with heavy metal poisoning and her body was starting to degrade. Her life was teetering on the edge of death. She was about to give up the ghost and then she met Okami, and in a way Okami nursed her back to life, teaching her this work. She said that even though she had studied energy work through martial arts, it was this work that really had saved her.

Each week that Joon and I met, our work deepened and my ability to read became stronger and clearer. I discovered that our weekly healings were almost a psychic synopsis of the inner work I had been doing between sessions. The farther we went along, the more the work took on a life of its own.

At some point after over a year of doing our clearing work, Joon said she was going to travel and recommended I contact Okami for the next steps. I reached out to Okami and she said that she had people I could work with. She eventually introduced me to a few of them. One was a woman who was a schoolteacher; another was a man who was a chiropractor and traveled with celebrities, doing holistic healing and energy work on them; and another was a woman who was a dancer. I practiced individually with this group of people over an extended period time, learning to work with different people who embodied different energies. This refined my ability to read varied energies. I learned through working with these individuals that people can bring a whole different style of seeing and feeling energy into their work. I learned that as humans we are very magical creatures with deeply individual gifts and connections.

Okami called me one day to ask how I was doing. I told her about the many profound impacts of working with the blue flame.

She said, "Have you ever seen a picture of the Medicine Buddha?"

I said, "No."

She said that I should take a look. I went to a store that had posters of varied Buddhas. I came across one that was brilliant and deep blue, the color of the flame of transformation and healing. It was the Medicine Buddha. I bought the picture and placed it in my healing room where I did clearings.

CHAPTER TEN
THE DIAMOND

One day after my initial healing classes with Okami had finished, I went to visit Mathias. I thanked him for sending me to Okami. He asked how it had gone. I shared everything she had taught me.

He listened attentively and said, "You know, even the simplest meditation is just as powerful as the most complex." He held out his palm. He drew the shape of a three-dimensional diamond, like two pyramids on top of one another. He said, "When you meditate on the light above, the light below, and the light of the four directions and you connect them all in straight lines of light you get a diamond. A diamond is strong and impenetrable. If you are at the center of a diamond you might find your ability to travel within subtle realms clarified and inwardly magnified."

He got quiet for a moment. "There are many who live in the woodwork of the world who you can work with and practice healing on who have also learned different types of healing techniques."

Mathias said he wanted to share a story with me. A few days earlier as he was driving by a school, he psychically saw a child pulling out a gun and shooting another child. It disturbed him enough that he went home and meditated on it. He saw the image of the event appear and then slowly brought the image into the light until it shifted. He said that a week later a boy was caught with a gun in the school where he had seen the vision. He looked at me piercingly. "This doesn't mean you are doing some action, or looking for problems, but if Spirit shows you something sometimes it is good to move it into the light."

Not long after Mathias shared that story with me, I was on a bus traveling through South Seattle. I was meditating on the bus and I opened my eyes to see a young child and his mother in front of me. In meditation, I felt an unusual energy building inside of me, a strong light building from within my heart. The light continued to build and then moved outside me, not of my own accord, and surrounded the child sitting in front of me. A few seconds later there were some extremely loud bangs and I could see blue flashes in front of the bus. It dawned on me that someone was shooting a gun in front of the bus.

A young man was shooting across the street. I was strangely calm, and everyone ducked. The shooter was maybe two feet in front of the bus. Luckily, no one seemed to get hurt and the bus drove off. I was a little shaken after this experience but still relatively calm for having seen a shooting. I reflected on Mathias's words that the light sometimes happens on its own accord, and all we need to focus on is doing the work and allow it to run through us – just being a conduit.

Sometime later I attended another of Mathias's classes. Also attending the class was a younger man in his 30s named Jared. Jared worked as a businessman. I sat in on the class, more as an observer. Mathias asked me to just observe and said that learning would take place through my ability to simply be present. He asked me not to say anything during the class, which I found odd, but he had a glint in his eye so I assumed there was some lesson in it for me.

Mathias was teaching Jared some meditation techniques, but Jared seemed a little uncomfortable the whole time. After returning for a couple of classes, Jared confessed to Mathias that he was having a very hard time meditating at home. Mathias asked if he knew why and Jared said he didn't have a clear picture. Rather than telling Jared what was blocking him, Mathias had him go into meditation and look at what was happening to his energy. Jared came out a bit shaken. He revealed that what he saw was that his employers who were executives were abusing their power and treating people very badly. He said that he was a lower-level executive and he saw how he was not living in integrity in his current job by participating in the organization. He felt deep conflict inside himself as he didn't want to leave his job, but he saw in this meditation that his spirit had been screaming at him to get away from these unhealthy characters. This was the root of his inability to meditate – he didn't want to see just how much stress his subtle body was absorbing.

Mathias then spoke about his own life, explaining that he worked with some very heavy characters in his jobs. As if assessing his next words carefully, he said, "When we stop giving our power away in situations it can shift the entire group dynamic. This can be particularly clear when we work in an office. It can also be deeply uncomfortable for those around us who don't want to see the reality that they are hurting others. This can create new dynamics where people in our vicinity won't want to see themselves if they aren't in integrity. This causes us to become a larger and shinier mirror for those not living in integrity, causing them to want to run or react against their own reflection. This can also be seen as a magnification of their behavior that is lacking integrity."

He then said, "I might surmise that you are afraid of your light. Because if you were meditating you would be deeply in power."

Mathias mentioned to Jared that he might want to do some inner work in his past relating to pleasing others. He insinuated that this aspect of him was fighting against his peaceful and powerful aspect, but that only he could attest to that. Jared shook his head in full acknowledgment and seemed to be deep in his mind, reflecting.

Mathias continued, "This might be a good time to look at the role your father played in this dynamic." Jared again nodded as if he understood.

I could see tears in Jared's eyes as he said, "I see how I can get my power back. By simply being in my light within myself. So very simple, yet not."

I felt chills as he spoke, and I got the feeling that Jared's father had done some hard things to him. I just watched and held space and presence for him as Mathias had instructed. By the end of the session, Jared had a new glow; a pronounced shift had taken place within him. For me, I got to experience yet another aspect of this powerful work I was doing with Mathias.

Later Mathias approached me and said, "Sometimes in groups of people, one person will face something that no one else can or is ready to face. In that instant, everyone receives healing and opening of awareness."

He looked at me and asked if I understood. With a glint in his eye he said, "I asked you to come to the class with Jared as Spirit told me you needed to be there to experience what Jared was going to see and heal."

I said, "I see the similarity to myself, giving my power away to people in authority." He smiled and nodded. "You're always safe when you are centered in yourself and you are always powerful as your true Self."

Around this time, meditating had become a full inner and outer life experience for me. My meditations often happened during the hours that I was moving around and going about my daily life; I didn't need to be sitting in meditation to be in meditation. Mathias had taught me to activate my light systems by simply forming an intention and flipping a switch. After so many years of being connected to this light, this process had become second nature.

Mathias had mentioned a diamond. In meditation one day, I went inside it. I saw my connections to the lights above and below, and I saw lights connecting them to the four directions to form a perfect diamond of light around me. As I held this space there was an opening, like standing at a clear doorway. What was beyond that I would find out later.

CHAPTER ELEVEN
THE SILENCE

After a long break of not seeing Mathias, one day he invited me again to his home. It was a warm spring day and as I arrived, I looked up to see multiple hawks silently circling above his home, flying in spirals. One was so high I could barely see it. I stood and just stared for a long time, watching them swirl in the ether of the sky.

After we were settled inside, Mathias said he had a new lesson. He sat across from me, staring at me expressionlessly for what seemed like forever. After what may have been 10 minutes, I found myself getting very uncomfortable as he sat and stared. I began laughing and squirming around while looking back at him. I didn't know what to do with him not saying a thing and him being so quiet. He continued staring, motionless and expressionless, completely silent.

After going through many inner conflicts, I finally closed my eyes and started to meditate in silence. I immediately relaxed and sank extremely deep into that quiet. For a moment I opened my eyes and Mathias had also closed his eyes, so I sank back into the meditation. We sat in silence for what seemed like an hour. All my insecurities dropped away after the initial inner turmoil merged in the silence. I saw how the quiet brought up every issue I wasn't looking at in the moment.

I eventually opened my eyes and he was looking at me, smiling. He quietly said, "All the techniques in the world mean little in the presence of silence. Being silent brings it all together, into the now. Anytime you are unsure about a situation in life, simply be silent and it will help everything become clear."

He stood up, escorted me out, gave me a hug, and I left.

I went home and felt a deep quiet inside, like I had taken a much-needed inner rest. All I wanted to do was be quiet. I sat for my usual mediation and instead of doing all the techniques for healing, I simply sat in silence. After this experience, on my own accord I decided to dedicate one day a week to not talking and being in silence. I found it deeply profound and helpful. Some days I would use techniques and some days I would simply set an intention for silence in my meditation. Arranging my days to fit into this schedule was challenging at first. Getting used to not taking phone calls was a little tricky, and arranging my days so I didn't go to places where I would need to talk to others took some time, but after the patterns became more comfortable it became a lot easier. As this pattern got more set, the days of silence became deeply peaceful and I began to really look forward to my quiet alone time. I didn't own a television, so much of the time was spent with my own thoughts, cleaning, walking, or meditating.

The next time I visited Mathias at The Sage, I was standing over the railing looking at the alley with him and he said, "Sometimes when I sit in meetings with people who are in charge of the foster care system I can see psychically that someone is speaking dishonestly about situations concerning the children. As I see this intuitively, I simply focus on the truth and I get deeply silent. Not just silent on the outside but on the inside. As I patiently wait and focus on the truth in silence, the person either reveals their dishonesty or gets really upset and leaves the meeting, revealing their true agenda. Silence is very powerful for revealing the truth, both inside you and outside you."

He told me to practice it in situations where people were being dishonest or challenging. "The secret of silence is to be in the quiet with intention but without tension."

I took this lesson into my work. One day, while working at a center with children, there I noticed a particular child and sensed something was a little off. I listened inside. My intuition clearly stated that something bad was happening at home to the child. When the parent arrived, I found my entire system on edge, reacting in a very direct way. I decided to practice the technique of intending silence. This silence kept me from overreacting and kept me clear in my mind. Soon the truth was revealed – there was an issue at home and the child was put in a safer situation.

In another situation, I was working with a child who had been removed from a parent after being physically abused. The child had many challenging behavioral problems and the mother found it very difficult to find anyone to care for the child. I spent a lot of time with this child and one day I felt a change in the air. The child was in a particularly bad mood and was doing things to hurt others. I got deeply silent inside and just stayed present. As the day went on, the more the behavior got out of hand. Finally, I calmly had to usher the child into another area for the protection of others.

This particular day the calmer I got the more aggressive the child became until at one point the child started shaking and yelled at me in full force, "Just hit me Andy, just hit me!"

He then burst into tears. He was only five. I looked him in the eye and said I would never hurt him and that I deeply cared about him. I told him that people who care about each other treat each other gently and kindly. I gave him a big hug. After that the child's behavior completely changed; it was like night and day. He knew that I wasn't going to react; my silence had facilitated that. The poor child was simply looking for love. He had always just been looking for love and was expecting to get hit in return. It was a profound moment for me with the recognition that being loving, patient, and silent is deeply healing when one works with children. It would be healing in any situation in life, but this day it was particularly powerful.

In another instance, I worked with a young girl who would go into fits of screaming and yelling. She had been adopted and no one knew how to deal with the situation when she started screaming. When I was with her and this would happen, I would get deeply silent and simply be present. I would center and quietly activate all my inner light systems, and then I would just be with her. When episodes would happen, I would intuitively see the child reverting to some deep time period when she was a baby. I could see her in my mind's eye fully dissociating, replaying her trauma over and over. The more I was present and loving with her without reacting, the more the episodes calmed until one day they just slowed to a stop. Presence and absence of judgment with inner silence help hold a space of love. Silent love should have no pretext and no expectations.

I realized that people are often judged for their deep pain that is projected onto their reality. Understandably people get upset if they are attacked, but if someone in their life chooses to present them with love and are truly present for them it is deeply healing. Over time the awareness dawned in me that trauma is multilayered pain piled on top of itself, with people self-creating more and more issues until the they collapse within themselves. This can be reflected in people who turn to drugs to numb the pain, or who are so burdened all they can do is lash out and abuse others to feel relief. Yet, underlying it is simply a wounded child. We are all just wounded beings that at some point need a reminder that we are loved and that we are love. All the people in prison, and in prisons of their own making, are simply in need of presence. Over time I realized that the power of silence is simply the power of love.

Mathias told me that with all the intuitive power one has, it can actually make things more difficult to navigate day-to-day life. One day he was working with a man and he saw an immense dark energy around his head. He said psychically he saw him commit a violent crime. Mathias said all he could do was remain silent and witness, even though he was witnessing quite horrific scenes and even feeling them deeply. He said it was not that unusual to witness strong energies in one form or another and I would need to get strong in my silence, in my presence, and in my centeredness. As time went on, I understood this to be true as I intuitively began seeing more and more in situations.

I also slowly began to understand that I was to keep all of it to myself in the silence unless someone asked. I was not to attempt any healing unless I was asked, and I was not to react. This was the strength gained from inner silence.

CHAPTER TWELVE
IN THE WORLD, NOT OF IT

Mathias said that he had a new student and asked if I would be interested in sitting in on the class.

I said, "Of course I would be. When have I ever said no?!"

***

As I arrived Mathias told me he wanted me to participate but as in the past, he asked me to hold a quiet and aligned energy. He wanted me to simply hold space.

His home was so comfortable, a familiar place for me. After settling in, a woman came in. She was tall and had a strong presence. Mathias asked us to introduce ourselves. I told her about myself and she introduced herself as Laila. She said she was a lawyer and had spent most of her career as a district attorney. She mentioned that her current role in the lawyer world was difficult and that Mathias had been helping her with some of her past childhood trauma. It was always intriguing to me how very different people appeared to Mathias, all being attracted to him for different types of healing. When Mathias started the class, he showed her the connections to light.

Each of Mathias's classes had a slight individual flavor, tailored just for the people present. With Laila, he led the meditation slightly differently, spending more time having her connect to her heart center and instructing her to connect to various colors.

At one point he turned to me and said, "Each of you has gifts. You, Andrew, are deeply elemental while you, Laila, are strong and expansive like the sunrise." His eyes were shiny and looking in the distance. We sat quietly for a long time absorbing his words.

Laila and I came back for more classes over time. She revealed she had been facing hard situations at work regarding racism. She had always had challenges with her job due to her sensitivity to energy but now she was facing straight-out racism, being the only African American in her company. She was being given more and more work, while being berated regularly. She was garnering the strength to possibly sue the company after coincidentally meeting another African American woman who had quit after experiencing the same situation. She said she was working on not running away, which she really wanted to do. She said it had been the hardest fight of her life and all she wanted to do was hide away but she knew, deep down, she had to face the pain head-on. She said Mathias was giving her tools to heal her past wounds as well as tools of strength.

I was in awe of Laila's strength and power to face these challenges. They sounded so painful and it really opened my eyes to deeper levels of what others go through on a regular basis. I had never suffered discrimination, and I couldn't imagine being a lawyer, much less an intuitive lawyer who had to fight every day in this way.

In class Mathias said, "The strength is not in the fight but in the light."

He explained, "You simply needed to find the strength to be unwavering. If you clear the inside, the road to the outside will get easier.

"I had to deal with something similar in my past... I was fired from a job due to discrimination. This incident went all the way to the Supreme Court. I did my best to not give into fear or reaction but held as steady as I could through the proceedings. I centered with intention, listening to my inner Self for direction, and I followed through on all the actions I needed to take. The case was won, and I felt clear to simply move on after the fact. This doesn't mean I didn't feel terrible in both intuition and emotion while the proceedings were taking place, but I simply held steady inside my inner light, unmoved in my center, present to everything happening outside."

I listened to their stories in gratitude that I got to sit in on the process of healing that was taking place. Each time we meditated, Mathias had Laila focus on her heart, clearing the lower part of her energy, working on her heart and body. The gift was that I got to work on myself in similar ways in the class.

In a later class, Laila told Mathias that she had to go into surgery to remove a small tumor. Mathias asked her whether she needed to go into surgery or if she just needed to do some particular inner healing work around her childhood. Laila acknowledged what he was saying with a sort of exasperated look. Laila went home and did inner clearing. She then later told us that she had gone in for the surgery and during the process, the surgeon could not find the tumor. It had disappeared. This happened twice to her: the doctors found a tumor, she did some inner clearing, and the tumor disappeared. She said the doctors were dumbfounded.

Later, Laila mentioned to Mathias that she wanted to have a child but that she was having problems conceiving. She went to some of the top fertility doctors in Seattle, who all said that she would not be able to have a child. She told Mathias this and again he told her to do some inner healing work on it. She went into it and saw blocks in her reviews of her life. She cleared the way, and just as with the tumors, the doctors were dumbfounded when she got pregnant.

Before Laila had the child, Mathias had me go over to her home and do some healing work with her. It was a profound experience for me to feel both the child's and mother's energies together. A deep and profound awareness opened in me over the many sessions we did together, specifically in terms of how the higher Self and energy of a child lives and exists in the womb. I felt deeply grateful for the opportunity to be of service on this level as well as grateful for the deep, integrated learning that took place.

* * *

Mathias always stressed the importance of practice. "You can go to any number of healings, undergo endless transformations, or take any number of meditation classes, but none of it will last. It will all be temporary if you are not doing the inner work. Long-lasting, sustained healing must come from the inside. The whole point of our time together is to lead you to the healing of yourself. The results should ideally give you the ability to be more loving, comfortable, and present in your body no matter what experience you are having in the world."

At one point when I was with him at The Sage, he got that glint in his eye. "You know that sometimes people prefer to avoid conflict at all costs. They will go to any lengths to simply not address some issues."

He then gave me a serious look. "No matter what road a person travels within themselves they will never be free if they can't face the present moment."

He stayed quiet, looking at me for a long time. I let his words sink in. I knew he was referring to me indirectly and that I was the type of person who really didn't like conflict. I had never thought that avoiding conflict was averse to me doing the work.

He looked at me and said, "All these tools are here to help you confront what's standing in front of you, not avoid what's in front of you." For some reason the seriousness made us both burst out laughing. When we calmed down, I told him I understood.

I said, "It's about being fully in the world, but not of it." He nodded.

CHAPTER THIRTEEN
CLEARING

Mathias said that one of his clients was setting up a new business inside an older building on Capitol Hill, and he had asked Mathias to do a clearing on the space. Mathias wondered if I would like to participate in the clearing. I told him, of course, I would. I didn't really know what it meant to do a building clearing, but I was very interested.

When I arrived at the new business space, Mathias told me to simply get connected and hold space and light, and that my presence would be very helpful. Mathias went through each room of the business and started reading the energy in a similar fashion to the way Okami taught me prior to doing a clearing on a person. He pointed out where trauma had been locked in from the past. He showed where people had left issues of neglect or abuse in the building and explained how he saw the energy had been stuck.

After getting to a root problem and appearing to unhook it, he would sweep his arms while blowing to clear it. At the same time, he asked me to put my hands on the walls and to imagine light running through the walls. We went room by room clearing the business until we had brought light to every space. Finally, he had the new owners come in and stand in a circle with me and him. He asked them to close their eyes and imagine all the things they wanted for their new business. He told the couple that he and I would magnify the energy while they spent time focusing their feelings and wishes into space, magnifying them in light. I intuitively felt the new owners' desire for clients, a desire for a community, for wealth, and for a fun, active community place.

Mathias then told them he was going to add the last piece. He sat deeply quiet, not explaining what he was doing. Then, he smiled and told them he was all done. The business was going to open the next morning at 8 a.m. Mathias and I later found out there was a line of people waiting for the brand-new candle shop to open, which was profound because it was not a busy location, slightly off the main street.

One day not long after, Mathias again asked me if I would like to do a clearing, this time in the apartment of one of his students. We went to the person's house and we immediately both felt that a lot of heaviness had happened in that space. Mathias asked the person why she chose that apartment to live in and she said it had been passed down to her from a friend. She mentioned that she and her friend both felt that there was a darkness about the place, sometimes having terrible dreams. As we stood there, I had a foreboding feeling.

Mathias noticed my feelings and energy and sharply looking at me said, "Don't dive into the fear. It is not yours."

That immediately took me out of the feeling. Mathias started to read the past to do the clearing. It was a small, one-bedroom apartment. He started in the bedroom and said at one point that people who had lived there stored guns, a lot of guns, in the closet, and that they had criminal and abusive tendencies. He saw someone locked in a closet. I tried to maintain my balance and inward focus on my light systems.

He said that at one point someone's head had been banged against the wall in a fight, leaving a hole in the wall; through his psychic sight he said that they never repaired the wall — they just put wood paneling over it. He knocked on the wood paneling right where he said he saw the person get smashed into the wall, and it was hollow. He then knocked next to it, and it was solid. The woman at this point was clearly mind-blown at Mathias's abilities. I also felt she was slightly horrified by all the information.

Mathias cleared the energy and had me put my hands on varied walls, focusing on running light through them. As I did this, he talked about the layers of abuse vibration that existed in the apartment and how he saw it layered over many people living there, person after person. He asked the woman if she had felt more aggressive since living there and she said yes. She mentioned she had been in more arguments with people than usual since moving in.

As if talking to Spirit itself Mathias then said loudly, "We are going to clear all this off and brighten this up!"

I felt a chill, as I rarely heard Mathias raise his voice.

Just as we did with the business clearing, we continued holding light and eventually had the woman focus on what she wanted for her home and how she wanted it to feel. We magnified that energy throughout the house. Afterward, she said it felt like a brand-new home, as if we had energetically bleached the structure.

* * *

Later, I went to visit Mathias at The Sage. Standing over the alley in our regular spot, he looked piercingly at me and I thought to myself, "Oh, here it comes!" Mathias laughed loudly, clearly reading my thoughts.

After composing himself he said that sometimes when he was out in nature, the surrounding land would ask him to run certain energies, and that sometimes he was asked to clear old or even ancient pain off the land that had been left by humans as trauma. "Nature is her own cure; we just speed up the process of healing."

I asked him how he cleared a whole area of nature when it was outdoors, and he said I already knew how to do it.

He said, "I simply enter a deep state of being, that was taught to me, that was taught to you." He smiled.

He said he connected to the light above and below, while making sure he was surrounding himself with light. He then placed himself in a deep position, guided by Spirit entirely in the moment.

"Spirit guides you into what you need to do with light, with the elements. You simply need to follow the inner movement and prompts."

He then said, "I clear the energy that is shown to me, sometimes using elemental energy, sometimes using different bands of light, and I go to the root and unhook the deep block in history, like I would with a person. Sometimes this may look like standing in the flame of transformation or standing under a waterfall of energy from the Universe above."

He said, "If someone were not energetically ready to do this type of clearing, it could be quite dangerous. I recommend that you only do it when truly called or asked clearly by a person or Spirit. Spirit will show you when it is time."

"There is a reason I am telling you this now. I am being called into the mountains and I thought of asking if you had an interest in going."

I responded that surprisingly I had felt a desire to take a trip to the mountains recently. He said, "Surprisingly?" then laughed.

The next day we drove east of Seattle up into the mountains, sitting fairly quiet, meditating through the trip. Over the course of the drive, a large number of hawks flew over the car, to the point where I lost count. As always in Mathias's presence, I felt a deep feeling of well-being.

Mathias interrupted the silence and said, "Sometimes before a class or big healing session my body aches deeply, I feel pressure, and it can feel like a dark cloud overhanging the mind."

He stayed quiet for a moment and then continued, "I tend to feel things to my bones, and with that comes maintaining a certain stability, all the while navigating the deep energies and emotions of others. To be honest, this is something I have had to navigate my whole life, since I was a deeply intuitive child.

"Before a clearing, you may be starting the healing work before you even arrive. You may intuit the pain that is arising through the healing that is about to occur." Not surprisingly Mathias's words reflected how I had just started to feel. A heaviness had appeared, a foreboding feeling, with a sort of weight on my shoulders and head.

He continued, "As you know some people feel and some people see, and those who feel are often like, 'Get that crap away from me!'" He laughed.

"People who psychically see are often fascinated with their visions. They are like, 'Whoa, let me take a look at that interesting thing, let me bring it closer and closer so I can see it,' while the "feeling" psychics start yelling to keep it away, because it feels absolutely terrible."

He added, "It is important for the seers to not get fascinated and the feelers to not avoid. It is important to get to know what you are feeling and seeing through practice. Your system knows what is happening. Breathing and maintaining centeredness are deeply important."

Mathias said he wanted me to guide us to where we might stop. I felt an urge to pull off the highway and enter a side road. As we drove, the road followed alongside a beautiful river, eventually turning into dirt. We ended at an area with a couple of park benches deep in a mountain forest.

Mathias said, "What are you feeling?"

I said, "Suffering."

We got out of the car.

"What are you seeing?"

I hunched over feeling slightly overwhelmed, not really wanting to see what I was seeing.

Mathias said, "Just breathe," as he put his hand on my shoulder.

I said, "I see a line of people, Native Americans, all chained together here, women and children." I stood fully up to see exactly where they were standing in the past. It looked as if their Spirits were still there, chained. I could make out their faces and clothes.

Mathias said, "Why are we here?"

I told him what I saw and said, "I feel us here to bear witness to the trauma in the past, as it still exists because no one has taken responsibility."

As I acknowledged the energy, the past pain first shot deeply into my heart, a literal physical pain, and then a lightness started to come over my being.

I told Mathias, "The people here in this place were so connected to the elements, they were completely part of them."

I walked over to the river's edge and then saw spirits floating above the river, part of the water. I told Mathias that I was feeling we should meditate there on the river's edge. I felt Mathias's energy pushing me deeper into this awareness and deeper into my psychic sight. We sat down to meditate. I felt light coming through us and beginning to fill the river and the area where the people had been harmed. I felt relief and energetic shifting through the simple fact of bearing witness and the light moving through us. Mathias's energy was intense, and I could feel him moving deep energies under the earth we were sitting on.

Mathias and I meditated there for quite a long time. I then heard him get up and walk to the bench area. I slowly came out of meditation and went to find him. He was standing past the benches looking at something. I approached to see what he was looking at. It was a little sign that said, "In Memory," with the name of a tribe inscribed on it.

If I ever had any doubt about the work I was doing with Mathias, it was completely washed away at that moment. The depth of suffering was overwhelming and there was a deep acknowledgment within me of the pain that persists for generations, both within and outside us. To bear psychic witness to such pain was deeply overwhelming and intense. I recognized that the light we brought could not change things but ideally could bring a little healing to that area of planet Earth at that moment in time. There was also a clear acknowledgment within myself that although I felt that pain for an instant, I could never really know what it was like to be subject to such horror. I could only have compassion.

We drove home in silence. I felt a deep but clear grief at what had happened to the people but also deep gratitude for Mathias, who always followed his own guidance so clearly.

CHAPTER FOURTEEN
THE ADULT

One day, out of the blue, Okami contacted me and said she had intuited that I was ready for the next steps in healing work if I desired to continue. It had been a couple of years since I had last worked with her. I went to her home and was greeted by Vala. As we settled in, Okami asked me how my healing work was going. I told her the work had really opened me up to new levels of understanding and healing. I had gotten to a point where I felt confident doing past-life clearings. She then asked how the present-life healing work was going. I said I was able to clear issues often. If I felt triggered by something, whether in my external world or intuitively, or if a problem in my life were arising, I would either go to the cave of review that Mathias had taught me or into the past-life cave. I told her the two healings would sometimes overlap and merge together, yet remain separate.

She stayed quiet for a while and then said, "In reality, there is no need for the past-life clearings if someone is doing all their work in this life. Everything you need to access is given to you in this life."

She continued, "On occasion, all these various tools can be a distraction from what the main goal is. The goal is to heal what you've come to heal and to gain full presence and power in your life. The whole idea is to be embodied in this life, alive, vital, and free."

She then said she wanted to talk to me about becoming an adult.

"In the current culture of the United States, it is rare for someone to do a ritual on becoming an adult."

She asked me if I knew what she was talking about and I said I did not.

She said, "In many past cultures around the world, there were rituals that were performed when moving into adulthood. In many of those rituals the ties to one's parents were cut and the person then symbolically became an adult. In other words, they were tied to something grander than their birth parents."

She looked above her and said, "The representation of the cosmic mother and father figures becomes a greater reality when you symbolically become an adult. Many people are stuck in adolescence because they do not realize they are a child of the Universe…"

She looked at me and said, "Now might be a good time for you to write down on paper all the things you feel unresolved with your birth parents. Write them down as if you were writing real letters to them in a ritual fashion. I do not suggest sending the letters to them but simply write any focused, unresolved issues you may have. Then I recommend using your inner tools to allow yourself to fully become an adult, giving yourself grander freedom, a freedom that is gained through inner responsibility. This also gives your parents healthy freedom."

I went home and wrote down all the issues I could think of. I had already done a lot of work within myself concerning my parents, but I had never thought about the idea that I might be stuck in adolescence.

After some deep reflection, I saw a part of myself blaming my parents as the cause of some of my personal issues. This energy linked me to them in a way that kept me from growing into my adult self. I saw that underlying this blame were many instances where I was simply avoiding responsibility for my actions that led to a later negative result. This avoidance of responsibility kept part of me from being present in personal friendships and relationships. More simply put, I was simply dodging my ability to feel free to be responsible to myself. As I continued to dig into the hard issues in my letter, one area that I spent a lot of time on was my father and his addictions. These addictions caused a lot of pain for my mother, which filtered down to me when I was a young child.

I went into my cave of review. I breathed in many experiences with my father. My father was an actor, comedian, and entertainer who was able to make anyone in a room laugh. Along with that large and gregarious personality came a lot of partying. This partying often got him unintentionally into trouble. I spent a lot of time in deep meditation reviewing my life with him. As I wrote down all my issues and reflected in my cave, I slowly began to feel a shift in perspective, as if a light had opened through me. I could also see a light open into my dad's life, like a crack of light in the wall of an old house that I could peek through, and I saw how my father was adopted and how he was abandoned by his mother and father. I saw all these strands of energy that caused him to move toward more and more addictive behaviors. The more I delved into this, the more compassion I felt. This eventually led to a state of gratitude for the amazing man he was. He came from such a challenging situation and he made an incredible life for himself.

He followed his dreams, acted in movies, and sang to stadiums full of people. But mostly he had me.

I saw how the dynamics of his lack of commitment to my mother got passed down to me by the disaster of the divorce and separation. I had a constant longing for a father figure, and he left. That longing slowly turned to anger and resentfulness for not having him around, creating a lack of stability in my life. By the end of the process I felt a great weight had lifted off me and my family line.

Not coincidentally, a short time after this experience my father called me and asked to meet him. He said that he wanted to talk to me about some things. My father looked nervous when I saw him, which was unusual. We sat down at a coffee shop. He paused for a long time, looking fidgety. He told me that he had something serious to talk to me about. I listened as he told me that he had a gambling problem and that due to that gambling problem over the years he had gambled my college fund away. I listened and all I could do was feel compassion for him. After so much inner healing I felt I knew his struggles, maybe even more than he knew them. I did not get mad or upset but was present to his revelation and told him I understood. He apologized profusely. He said he was working on treatment for gambling. I told him I was proud of him for having the courage to share with me the truth and for seeking help. His face lightened up and he seemed relieved that I was non-reactive.

While meeting with my father I didn't realize that my response was due to the inner work I was doing. Only later did I fully realize how it had transformed my interactions with him. I used to adore him – he could do no wrong, and I idolized his every move even if it was destructive. Now, after doing this work with Okami, I saw him as an adult, clear and flawed, a human with real-life challenges. It was now easy to have a more wholistic compassion for him. He was a dynamic man with deep resources of creativity, and I could see his love for me through his personal challenges with sobriety. I easily forgave him because I understood his pain and his light.

CHAPTER FIFTEEN
THE CRONES

Okami said that she wanted to introduce me to a couple friends of hers, if I would be interested in meeting them. She said they lived far outside Seattle on an island deep in Puget Sound and that it would take a day of travel to get there. I said I would be very interested.

When the day came, Okami and I set out separately. I got on a ferry and spent the day traveling. Puget Sound, sometimes called the Salish Sea, is a beautiful place that I had always felt deeply connected to. I loved standing at the front of ferries watching over the edge as the large boats glided along the shiny, reflective water. As a child, I could always be found standing on the front deck feeling the cool wind rush through my being, energizing yet relaxing me.

After I got off the ferry, there was an extensive drive through a dark green forest. When I arrived at the house, I didn't know what to expect. Okami happened to arrive at the same time as me. As we greeted each other she said that today there would be a small gathering of healers. As I entered two women came to the door. We said hello and Okami hugged and smiled at them as if she had known them for a very long time.

One woman with noticeable red hair held out her hand and introduced herself as Neve.

She then introduced her partner, Enesta. They told me to make myself at home. They said the woman on the couch was Jan and that I should introduce myself. Jan was a lot older, maybe even in her eighties, with super shiny eyes. She waved me over to sit next to her.

I said hello and she smiled with a side grin and introduced herself. I got the feeling she was mischievous by her expression.

She blurted out so everyone could hear, "Welcome to the house of crones!" They all laughed hysterically. As Neve approached, she said, "Really though, we truly are the crones," And they burst again into laughter.

Neve and Enesta walked to the center of the room and started talking to me. They said that Okami had informed them that I had been doing a lot of healing work with her and that she felt they might be able to share some of their work on their own paths of healing.

Neve said, "We have been on this path for a long time. Beyond being life partners Enesta and I are a healing team. We work in energetic tandem and we spend a lot of time healing others when not in our day-to-day work lives."

She said that they often worked on the subtle realm, in meditation and in dreams.

They looked at me seriously. Okami, who was sitting on another chair, was also staring at me. I could feel the weight of their silence and their eyes on me as if they were focusing on my reaction to what was being said.

Neve continued and said that after a period of time of self-healing a shift had happened, and they slowly started being guided to do specific healing work with others.

Enesta then cut in. "I am often called in my dreamtime to help people."

She looked at Neve and said, "Just like last night."

Neve said to Enesta, "Oh yeah, when you went cold. It was particularly strong last night. I had to cover you with lots of blankets."

Neve looked in space and then at me and said, "Enesta and I tend to be opposites in energy. When she is doing dreamwork and deeply connected she exudes a cold energy like the Arctic all around her. I on the other hand exude heat like a desert. Last night, I woke to a deep cold in our bed, which is common when her spirit is called to do service work."

Enesta looked at me. "I was called to a terrible car accident where a family was in need of transition help, helping them cross the threshold by holding light."

This really piqued my interest and so I really zeroed into what they were saying.

Okami leaned toward me and said, "We will be covering some of this soon. Some people work entirely in the dream realm to help people cross. We each have our own gifts."

While Okami was speaking to me Enesta grabbed a large, beautiful fan off the shelf. It appeared to be made of hawk feathers. Enesta began to wave the fan.

She could see my interest in it, and she said, "I made this. I was shown in my dreams how to make it after finding a dead hawk that appeared on my path."

She waved it over herself as if clearing her energy and then walked over and then asked Okami to stand up. She waved it over Okami. Okami closed her eyes. I sensed that a powerful clearing was happening, Okami's face gave the impression of standing in a wonderful wind. After clearing Okami from head to toe she looked at me and said her Native American ancestors often came to her and guided her healing work, especially in dreams.

She nodded for me to stand and she cleared my energy with the fan. It felt like a wind rushing through me, sending chills to my bones. It put me in a deep altered state, and I stood there with my eyes closed, quite blissed out. I was unsure how long I was in an altered state, but I heard Jan stand up slowly. I watched as Enesta cleared Jan, and I perceived that this healing was working on many levels, clearing old pains, and I felt deeply grateful for the experience of feeling and seeing the work take place.

Enesta then grabbed a small hand drum off the wall. She started drumming rhythmically. Neve handed me a djembe drum and said that I could join in drumming if I wanted to. Jan nudged me to go ahead and take the drum, and then Neve grabbed another hand drum of her own. We started playing while Jan tapped the chair with her eyes glowing. I felt something move inside me and I started playing the drum deeper and more rhythmically.

Enesta came up to me, and I stopped playing and stood up again. She started drumming rhythmically above my head, then louder and louder as if drumming into my being. I felt the energy like a clear wave pulsing along my head and deep into the earth, and again it put me in an altered state. She then had Jan and Okami stand up. She drummed over their energy, clearing them with the drum.

After she finished, they asked if I would like to practice some of the healing work that Okami had been teaching me.

I said, "Of course."

They had Jan lie on the ground. As she slowly got onto the floor, she turned toward me and said that since she had started learning this type of work many, many years ago she had put her cancer in remission. Jan said that she could easily intuit that this work was natural to me and that she was in capable hands for me to do some clearing work with her.

Okami leaned over and said, "This is a perfect time for you to start taking guidance from within on healing work. I have shared with you many tools, but to listen to the inner movement of your own spirit is the best and clearest way to get to know yourself."

I acknowledged what she was saying and kneeled at Jan's feet. I closed my eyes, centered, and felt immediately moved to scan her entire energy field, from the feet up to her head. My hands slowly moved above her energy field. I felt light move through her system. As a stagnant point arose my hands would pause and I would see energetic hooks and unlock them, releasing them and seeing the leftover darkness transform into light. I could feel pain around her organs and saw it lift. I felt the presence of the three other experienced healers around me watching me, their energy helping and pushing the work deeper, almost as if they were working through me. As I moved deeper into her energy field, I saw with my inner sight Jan as a young child with an abundance of innocence and joy and how that had been compressed and darkened by familial abuse. I saw many layers of protection, thick like a turtle shell, lift off her inner child and as it lifted it merged into light within her. She let out a deep breath as if really letting it all go. I finished up by clearing her entire energy field with a sweep. Enesta then handed me the fan and I did one last gentle sweep of the energy with the fan, feeling chills of a subtle wind blow through the entire space. It felt like a true gift to use the fan for healing.

Jan took a long time to open her eyes, and then we all helped her up. She looked lighter.

She looked at me and said, "Thank you. I knew I was supposed to be here tonight."

She paused and then looked right at me and said, "In society, ego is common for young men. It is good if you try and keep yours in check. The deeper you strengthen your inner resources, the deeper your outer resources will be. Take this as the wisdom from the old crone," and they all burst into loud laughter.

I knew they thought it was funny but there was a deeper acceptance and power behind their laughs, a deep acceptance of themselves and a power in age and wisdom that they all exuded.

I traveled back home on the ferry to Seattle floating on Puget Sound under the clear, white moon illuminating the dark ocean. With the moon infusing the sky with her light I felt a deep inner magic carried from this experience. I sent my gratitude in light in all directions. I arrived home renewed and inspired.

CHAPTER SIXTEEN
THE DISTANCE TO HERE

I went to visit Mathias at The Sage. Like so many times before he was standing in his usual spot, like an eagle overlooking the alley, overlooking the world. He smiled when he saw me, and like spreading his wings he gave me a big hug. He said he could sense that I had been busy and that my subtle energy had been very active. I told him about the experience with the crones. He laughed and found it amusing.

We started a conversation but in mid-sentence, he stopped and looked off in space. He said it was time for a new lesson. He said that I had learned to journey within myself, but it was time to learn to journey from inside to outside more deeply. He said he would like me to travel that night to his home in subtle body form. He said he would leave an object for me to see, placed strategically in his home. He gave me the exact time and said that I should travel there from my own home in meditation. He said he would help me with this process, which would be a new opening.

I went home and felt a little anxious as I waited for the time to come. I decided to meditate beforehand. I connected with all my light systems, centering in the light above and below, journeying with the animal light, as well as the five-element lights and the directions, and then in the center of the diamond of light.

As the time got close, I felt a deep quiet, like a new energy building inside of me. It was quieter than normal. Then, as if someone had taken my arm, I felt pulled outside myself, across the city. I was pulled into Mathias's home. Everything was streaming with energy, like waves of light, and I saw Mathias sitting in meditation with a brilliant white light streaming all around him. I then saw another Mathias standing next to a table with glowing eyes, even more brilliant than the one sitting in meditation. He reached out and grabbed my arm. As he grabbed my arm, my perception became vastly clearer. It felt as if he were sharing his energy to help me. This boost of energy awoke a part of me. I was standing in his living room and he pointed to an object on the table. It was a brilliant green. It had so much energy around it that it was hard to make out what it was. I got very close and saw what looked like a large green crystal. I stared at it for a very long time. After a while, I turned again to see Mathias staring at me with streaming lights coming out of his eyes. Without my volition, I was pulled back into my body and I could feel my form again.

The next day I went to visit Mathias. He asked how it had gone for me. I told him all I had experienced. He just listened, with his piercing gaze fixed on me. I told him that I had seen him in his body and in his subtle form and how much brighter he was in subtle form. In a flash of light, I saw his subtle form right in front of me. I went back and forth between the two experiences as I stared at him, and his energy drove the experience deeper, clarifying these two separate energies. I could see two of him at once.

After some silence, Mathias said, "I know you've known for a while, but this should clarify deeply that if you need my help, you don't need to see me in person. Just close your eyes and ask."

I stared at him for a while. I resisted what he was saying a little bit. I felt an unusual unease about not needing to see him in person. He noticed my resistance and asked me at what point in my past had I come to believe the world was so rigid and solid. I again stayed quiet for a long time. Intentionally, he pushed it deeper. "There is no need to see me in person. You understand this, right? These bodies are so limited."

I told him that as amazing as it was, it felt like a sort of loss, like I was going to lose someone important to me.

His eyes glowing, he said that the exact opposite was happening and that I was about to gain something extraordinary. He then burst into laughter and said, "Extra...ordinary."

This shifted the energy and caused me to laugh loudly. Mathias said it was so important to check our egos, our perceptions, and our power.

"We must always see our flaws and acknowledge that we are so deeply human. This acknowledgment helps you become more connected and helps you maintain integrity on the subtle plane. It is difficult to expand on the subtle when you are contracted and hiding things about yourself, pretending to be this or that. This is why the inner reviews and clearings of our past lives are so very important. Clear the way, clear the subtle body, clear the emotions, free yourself! And then your ability to travel will be unlimited..."

He added, "I am always here if you need me. There is no distance to here." He said this as he pointed to his heart.

"Simply practice, practice, practice."

I took the time to practice traveling. I was careful to be respectful, as in this kind of work, one can go and be anywhere.

It was quite liberating as there was no place on Earth a person could not go, both inside and outside. As I practiced, I also had the realization that there was actually no limit to time.

* * *

Not too long after I had received these lessons from Mathias, Joon contacted me. She was back from her world travels and wanted to know if I would like to practice more past-life clearing. I said of course I did, and we got together a few times for clearings. After a few sessions, I told Joon about my recent work with Mathias.

After listening closely Joon asked if I wanted to try past-life clearing work from a distance. I was kind of dumbfounded as I didn't even think that was possible. As she talked, it slowly dawned on me that really anything was possible from the inner world. After all, I had sometimes seen my own destiny, which astounded me.

We set up a specific time. One of us would be the client and the other the healer, and then we would switch and pick another day for the following session. As Joon had done this before she started as the healer. The time approached, and I meditated for an hour before we were due to begin.

When the exact time came, I immediately felt Joon standing next to me in subtle form. I was lying flat and I kept my meditation going. I could distinctly feel her moving up my energy field, clearing the energy. I felt twinges when it was being unlocked. This continued for maybe 30 minutes, and then the energy subsided and I could tell she had finished.

I called Joon to tell her about the experience. She told me that there had been a lot of energy around feeling confident, and she had cleared blocks to feeling self-confidence through my entire subtle body. I was in awe at what she was saying because it completely lined up with what I was seeing during my clearing. Flashes of situations when I had felt a lack of confidence passed over my mind. These included times I had felt fearful based on past experiences. One flash was seeing my teenage years when I was a singer in a band. We were performing in front of my whole school and all of a sudden the mic went out. I felt so ashamed and fearful to be in front of others after that experience, layering this fear and shame under false pretenses. I had flashes of past lives where I felt humiliated by others. I also saw layers upon layers creating a false sense of confidence as a survival mechanism for my insecurities.

It was now Joon's turn to receive healing. I got into meditation, made all my connections to the above and below, to the four directions, to the elements. I inwardly seated myself in the pristine diamond of light and when the time came, I saw Joon on my third eye screen. Using the simple intention of placing myself there, I found myself standing in a room of her house. She was lying on an ornate carpet. I was seeing everything as energy, so it appeared as if streams of light were coming from everywhere.

I came close to Joon and saw myself reach my hands out over her energy. I did the clearing just like I would in the physical world, and it felt just the same. I felt the shift when I saw each lock and hook and I felt the relief after clearing. The common theme that was prevalent with the lives that I was seeing was a consistent pattern of her fighting. I saw a psychological need for fighting in order to get things in life rather than the ease of allowing life to come to her. I cleared lock after lock of fighting for life, security, and success. When I finished, I saw Joon as a glowing white light, clear and content. I came back into my body and came out of meditation.

I called Joon not too long after and she confirmed everything I had been seeing. She said that lately she had been feeling the need to fight to get what she wanted, and that it was a pattern in her life. She realized during the clearing that flowing and ease with the Universe would help her create more of what she desired in this life.

I was deeply appreciative of this experience and thanked her for helping me learn how to do it. We started doing this regularly and the more we did it the more the themes of healing became stronger.

* * *

After many sessions with Joon, I contacted Okami to tell her what we had been doing. Okami said that at a certain point we might notice the past-life clearings becoming more universal. She said that some people even think that the clearings are taking place in a consciousness beyond our individual selves. She said that our karma is our own but that at some point the oneness of everything interconnects us all, especially on the subtle plane.

She said, "It becomes a service to everyone, almost as if we are clearing the world." She paused for a moment and then continued, "Because we are the world."

She looked off in the distance as if assessing what to say next. She smiled and said, "You know Mathias and I don't talk much in person these days, but we are in communication a lot."

I understood what she meant, and I told her she was lucky to have someone on that level to connect with.

She said, "When service of others is needed from us and asked of us, we do our best."

I asked, "What does service mean?"

She said, "When you are surrendered to your higher Self, the work is automatic and becomes service. An example of this is when you prepare to do healing work and your hands are guided and moved to specific places for healing. It is just like that but on a more encompassing level. It is by deep surrender that you are drawn to what is asked of you."

CHAPTER SEVENTEEN
DREAMING AWAKE

I woke from a long and clear dream. I was floating above an old friend and she was pregnant. I leaned over to her belly and I saw a light begin to glow. In this dream, I used the light from inside me and above me to help this being of light come out of her belly and move into the next realm. I was talking to a child in this light, saying everything was going to be okay. I felt a sense of sadness and relief when I woke. The dream was so clear and so impactful that I decided to go visit the friend who I dreamed about. She was an old friend from high school who worked at a coffee shop in downtown Seattle.

About a week later I went to the coffee shop. She was behind the register. I told her it was great to see her. I said that I had dreamed about her and would really like to tell her about it. She said she was about to go on break and would love to hear the dream.

We sat on the back steps of the store, in a quiet alley. As I told her my dream her eyes got big and then filled with tears. After listening to the whole dream, she became so emotional that she put her face in her hands and began weeping.

After calming, she said that she had not told anyone, but she had gotten pregnant and had lost the baby a week ago, the same time that I had the dream. She thanked me for telling her and she felt like I had somehow helped the spirit of her baby transition into the next realm. I was in awe at the way the whole scenario played out and felt deeply grateful that my dream had helped her.

I decided to go and tell Mathias about it. Mathias listened quietly as usual. He looked off in the distance and said that sometimes we do healing work in dreams and that for some it is a special ability. He said some even do healing work with others all night.

He had me close my eyes. As I began to meditate he had me make all my connections to the light, elements, and directions. He then guided me to my third eye screen. As he guided me, he said, "See your third eye screen there. On that screen I want you to see a recent dream you had; any dream will do."

I saw on my screen a dream I had of a coworker and how they were cooking food in my kitchen, serving me breakfast.

He then said, "Allow a higher aspect of yourself to interpret this dream and give the meaning on the screen."

I saw the images change into colors, and then into words that connected to substrates of energy in my mind. These words were "caring" and "comforting." I saw that the images were simply my mind's way of projecting images and interpreting caring energy that was flowing through my energetic experience.

Mathias said, "If you have any problems interpreting the images, see them become lighter, less dense, transitioning more and more into energetic symbols. See how the dream becomes lighter and faster."

Giving me some time to explore this he then said, "See how the dreams are your own higher Self speaking to you…

See how all the images you receive are your own higher Self speaking to you…"

He continued, "Now on that third eye screen see a short memory of your present life. Any memory will do. Imagine now for a moment that this memory of your life was a dream you were having. When seeing and feeling it as a dream, let it come into light more and more. See it become more energetic and symbolic as it transitions into the light, and notice how similar this experience is to the dream you just interpreted."

I brought up a memory of me driving on a highway, listening to the radio on an overcast day. I let the image slowly lighten up and become energy. As I did this, I let the dream come to me as a message. It came to me as simple energy without words, so I interpreted the feeling of the energy rather than a specific word. The more I brought the image into light the deeper it transformed into energy. At that moment I recognized the memory was not separate but part of me, in the same way that I don't see dream images as occurring outside myself. I saw my daily life as a symbolic message, a waking dream. This felt very deep, and it was very clear that if I practiced this, I would see my entire waking life as a collection of moving symbols or archetypes.

I sat in that profound experience in meditation for an extended period until I heard Mathias's voice quietly say, "It's time to come out of meditation."

I slowly came out, opening my eyes with a clear and profound awareness that this life was a lot more malleable and temporary than I had ever thought.

Mathias smiled and said, "When we meditate, we access deeper levels of understanding about ourselves. At moments in this training, we get a glimpse of deeper beauties that touch upon profound subtleties. Realizations come, letting us know that our entire reality is so small, yet so vast."

As if looking at the horizon, he said, "To dream-awake will help you awaken your dreams. The line when falling asleep becomes the line when waking up, and a whole realm of possibility can open up. This realm of possibility comes with another acknowledgment that your dreams and your reality are your very own higher Self. You may then notice that the light work you do in your nighttime dreams will increase exponentially. This is of course if you choose to use it as service to others – because as you just experienced, those others are simply your very own Self."

I went home to meditate on yet another profound reality shift.

CHAPTER EIGHTEEN
BEYOND ENDINGS

On our next visit, Mathias started talking about the fact that we don't have much of a ritual for death in our culture.

He said, "People tend to avoid this subject in thought and feeling. Though when people do focus on death in our culture it can become the polar opposite of avoidance, which is obsession. There is often a teeter-totter between these two. We can easily see this on the television programs Americans are obsessed with. Death and violence are the norm.

"More often than not it is an emotional and spiritual avoidance of the fact that our bodies are temporary and will eventually disintegrate back into the elements from which they came. One aspect of this work is to get comfortable with the temporariness of life, comfortable with our dissolution." He let his words sink in.

"Let me tell you a story. When I was younger, just beginning this work, I was spending some time with a close friend. I looked at him closely and I saw that his death was coming. I didn't tell him I saw death approaching but I did tell him it would be good to get his things in order. My friend looked at me a bit shocked and kind of brushed my suggestions away. A week later, this friend was at his birthday party and he got up to make a speech. He stood up and in a very dramatic fashion a little blood came from his nose and he fell over dead. The reason I share this with you is that today we are going to talk about death and we are going to do some work around the boundary between this world and the next, which may provide you with the ability to intuitively see people's approaching demise."

He continued, "The more comfortable you are with the idea of your own death, and the more you understand the meaning of it for yourself, the clearer you will be able to see it in the external world. In many ways, death is not something to fear but is one of your greatest friends." He let his words sink in, again.

"Reflection on death can help you make sound and calm decisions in the midst of chaos. Death is an utterly humbling friend and a truly calming influence. It can help you see that this life is ephemeral, less solid, and in reality, simply a dream we are having. From one dream to the next we shed the body and our soul jumps to the next one. In this work, we use light to see and acknowledge ourselves and all of our life and all of our experiences. This includes our demise." He stayed quiet for a moment.

"The more you face it, the more you will see that death doesn't really exist and that it is in fact just another facet of you."

He then told me another story. "There was a woman who got in a horrific car accident. She said when she crashed, she came out of her body. She could feel all the energy from all the people who were driving. The energy felt like a hundred little pinpricks of negative thoughts coming at her from all the cars in the traffic jam that the accident had caused. Hundreds of negative thoughts directed at her because they were angry and frustrated to be in a traffic jam. Then she could see that from a car far away a little light appeared. That little light turned into a fountain of brilliant light, like fireworks that overcame her and surrounded her, and she felt deep love and peace. While out of her body she was able to see the license plate of this car that the light was coming from. After being saved by paramedics she was taken to the local hospital. After waking she asked the cop helping her to find the license plate of the person whose car it belonged to. She went to the person's house and thanked the person for whatever they did. The person was shocked and said that while sitting in her car she had simply closed her eyes and imagined sending love and compassion to the people who were hurt, wishing that they were okay.

"It only takes one person. This is the power of light… This is the power of light…"

* * *

Mathias had a new student and asked if I wanted to sit in and help with the class. I said of course I did, as always. We met at Mathias's house and like usual his two dogs met us at the door. Mathias's home had become a sanctuary to me; when I went it was like entering a magical world and I had no idea what I would learn or what would happen.

When we arrived, I introduced myself to the new student. He said his name was John. John was tall, thin, and quiet. He had a shaved head and his presence was calming. He didn't share a lot during the class, but we covered some basics of working with energy while using light. Close to the end of the class, John mentioned that his grandmother had recently passed away. He said that his grandmother was a Cherokee leader in the southern United States; she was a spiritual leader and healer and guided not just her own tribe but many. He seemed deeply sad about it. Mathias listened carefully and said that he could see her next to him. John told us that in his tribe's tradition he had been initiated by his grandmother to be the next spiritual leader. He said that after one dies, the elder stays in a subtle body for a year to help the next generation.

Mathias gave an uncomfortable look and mentioned that her spirit was in pain. John said that he had not taken on the mantle of leadership that his grandmother wanted for him. He didn't want to leave the city, so she had come to the city to train him right before she died. Mathias said there was a lot for John to sort out within himself.

After a couple of classes with John, we became friends and would sometimes meet. Eventually, he became my roommate, so we spent quite a bit of time together. John would mention the struggle between his two worlds. He mentioned that when he was in the womb his grandmother pointed to his mother's belly and told his mother that he would be the next lineage holder. She said he would be a twin spirit, which was common for the healer leaders in his tradition. He said the problems occurred when his mother married a Christian man who took the family away from the tribe. He tried to make them give up their beliefs and so John was raised without the tradition of his family. He said that his grandmother came to Seattle many times to train him because he was the chosen one to play a specific role. She tried in many ways to convince him to come back to the tribe.

At varied times he would show me different aspects of his tradition and I felt grateful for the experience. He showed me how a traditional clearing was done with sage and an eagle feather. He shared with me a sacred box his grandmother gifted to him. This was particularly powerful because the purpose of the box was to initiate new leaders, and she was often called to various tribes to do the initiations. The box was used as a tool to assess the wisdom and development of the initiates. They were expected to put their hand in the box; if they could not, they were not mature enough, yet.

I would sometimes share with John a few of the things I was learning with Okami and he found it interesting. He said that in his tradition when someone was journeying with animals there would always be three animals that would come to them. It was always in threes, and the animal guides were not there to serve people; humans were there to serve the guides, as they were messengers of Spirit. He was very clear that people shouldn't try and control the messengers that come – to do so was a form of disrespect. I was grateful anytime John shared with me things from his traditions.

Another time, John was talking to me about people who we don't really want in our lives but we must engage with. He said his grandmother taught him a technique of visualizing mountain ranges growing all around oneself as a way of creating protection and distance. The larger the mountains, the more distance was created. I practiced this on occasion and felt it helped created a feeling of spaciousness, even if someone was sitting right next to me.

Inside, John struggled to listen to his grandmother, because he didn't want to take the mantle and it was eating away at his inner Self. Being split by worlds gave him an interesting perspective that impacted me and gave me a lot to reflect on. He eventually moved on to other adventures in his life, but he opened my eyes to a new spiritual and cultural experience. His work with Mathias seemed to be mainly helping him align with his grandmother and integrating that energy. Mathias was a conduit for the other side and so the work seemed dependent upon that.

In our sessions, Mathias spoke about holding space for those who were transitioning from this life. He said that we needed to be able to hold space for ourselves in order to be able to hold space for those who were passing away.

"To be present to the ancestors, to the beings on the other side, we need to be present to our own mortality. To hear the words of others you must be able to hear your own words; to feel the feelings of others means you must feel your own feelings. To talk to others beyond this world means that you can talk to yourself beyond this world," Mathias said.

My own father had been sick recently. His health was degrading as he battled heart and kidney problems. As his mental state declined a relative of ours had come by to see him and rather intensely told him that if he did not accept Jesus he would go to hell and suffer horribly. This caused a lot of unsettled feelings for my father, being that he was not clear in his mind from the medicines and illness. All the decisions he chose in his life came up to haunt him, and he feared he would be punished for poor choices or for being "evil." As his death approached, he became more uncomfortable and deeply feared what was next.

One day I sat at his bedside and asked him how he was doing. As I held his hand, he told me he was afraid. He was afraid because of what our relative had said. I got really quiet inside to listen to what the right response should be, and I told him about my near-death experience. I told him that death was an illusion and that underneath everything we were all just love and when we die we return to love. I told him that there was no afterlife of suffering unless we chose to be separate from love. Beyond the body, we were all just love. As I explained this to him the painful expression on his face slowly changed to one of ease. The wrinkle between his eyebrows lessened and he relaxed his body.

He was very sick but still very conscious when a doctor came into his room and told him he would not wake up the next morning. I held his hand, being present to this experience while he processed what that really meant. I stayed with him until he fell asleep. I sat next to him holding his arm until the last breath left his body. I meditated next to him and saw his spirit rise. I saw a pure light that he merged with. I felt the light and saw the ancestors standing in that light. I held the space in silence to make his transition smooth. In that moment I understood what Mathias meant by holding the light between worlds, holding steady between an illusory duality simply by holding space, holding love.

CHAPTER NINETEEN
THE MASK

Mathias often spoke about the need to assess ego in relation to one's humanness. He said that it was particularly important to reflect on one's own use of power on many different levels. If a person really wanted to progress in this work, self-checking one's own power was very important. As one takes greater and greater responsibility for their own behaviors, their energy, and their light they become clearer in energy. Mathias would often mention the necessity of assessing self-worth and self-importance in relation to beliefs about power.

He said, "By assessing power dynamics within ourselves we are assessing energies that influence our lives. Clearing away the debris, we begin to take more responsibility for our emotions and in essence our entire reality. You begin to gain clarity when you take more energetic responsibility, and with this clarity comes a melting between your inner world and your outer world. This melting eventually makes the personal mask in day-to-day life more fluid. This fluidity helps open you to new universal energies and experiences. One side benefit from this fluidity is improved physical health.

"If you can see where you may be having challenges in power as well as your worthiness you can access very deep resources. One way to do this is by placing yourself in challenging situations that test your ego. This can help you refine your edges. This refining can help you detach more and more from the personal mask you wear. The ego, the self-importance, the self-worth can be so easily tied up in the mask.

"Challenge the mask you are wearing, and you are challenging its reality. It has a life of its own. It often thrives on unconscious actions. Once you get clear on the mask, then you can free the energy from any role you play in life. If you are unattached to the outcome of the role, you are then freed on the inside, even while you act it out on the outside. As more awareness dawns around this, your mask moves closer and closer to the light, moving more into a dreamlike divine play where you are like an actor. Life then becomes like a play. It is one thing to say it; it is another to experience it. This is all done with inner work."

He paused for a while to let me really absorb everything he was saying.

He then continued, "This mask you wear is challenged in two ways: first by reviewing your life such as in the cave of review, breathing these experiences in and out, and then burning any issues into the white flame. Secondly, this mask is challenged by actually putting yourself in real-life situations that challenge the norm, that challenge the stability of who you are."

I asked him, "What does that look like? Do you mean to put myself in a challenging position?"

He said, "Find things that you personally judge and then move toward them to bring out the inner motivation that is stuck."

All this information still wasn't clear, which wasn't a surprise. Our conversations were so deep that I often didn't understand fully until I had spent time deeply reflecting on them.

As I reflected at home I sat wondering how and where I could challenge my ego in such a way. I assessed my current work. I enjoyed working with children, and in many ways they challenged my ego. Children have a tendency to refine someone's patience – if a person isn't already refined, they get burnt. Children teach adults how to be present and develop patience under any number of circumstances. Calm is necessary to be able to work with children. If there is a button to push, kids often find a way to lightly push it. This was definitely the case with me, and it often caused me to reflect and go inward – an excellent way to work on my own issues.

Yet, after assessing and meditating on Mathias's words there was definitely something missing in the challenge to myself. I liked to give things my all, so I thought I needed to challenge myself more than I was in working with children. I need to go full bore into burning my ego.

I began looking for a job that would challenge me and challenge me hard. My search was the opposite of what people look for in the normal American world. I looked for a job that would burn my arrogance to the ground. After a while I felt I had found the perfect one: working as a custodian at a busy hospital.

I jumped into it. The job was challenging and hard work. I would be called to any emergency cleanup while having my own specific area of the hospital to maintain. The area would change by the week, so I ended up over time rotating through the entire hospital, from surgery to emergency room to the neonatal unit. As I went along, I saw how people treated the custodians. People rarely talked to me and often the doctors wouldn't even acknowledge my presence. I learned that custodians kept the hospital running from the bottom up with not even a slight thank-you.

As time passed, I began to find a rhythm to the work. There was a meditativeness to the cleaning, sweeping, mopping, and wiping. Every time someone didn't treat me with respect, I would take it as an opportunity to wipe away a little ego. Every time I cleaned up something terrible, I thought about how it was helping people. The longer I did this job the more that the idea of what was important as a career changed. I valued the simple interactions with my fellow custodians, and I started to appreciate how people left me alone. After some time, I started to really enjoy it. The work became a moving meditation.

A few months into the job I visited Mathias. I told him I had quit working with children and was now working as a custodian at a hospital.

He asked, "Why did you do that?"

I said, "Because you said to challenge my ego." Mathias burst into laughter.

After composing himself he put his hand on my shoulder and said, "I just wasn't expecting that response. You always go full bore… This intense discipline you exhibit is definitely a multi-life characteristic of yours…" He paused as if assessing what to say next.

"It's true I said you should challenge your ego by putting yourself in places that make you uncomfortable. I honestly didn't expect you to make it your entire career." He laughed.

"What is most important is to challenge yourself in meditation, but now that you are here you do have a phenomenal opportunity to see the mask. You can really dig in and burn away some dross material that isn't needed. This will help open up energy that is needed to go deeper into your inner travels." I asked him if I was being too extreme.

He said, "You are your own judge of this. If you are challenging your ego then I imagine this is good, but if you are inflicting pain on yourself to prove your worth then that is another story. If you feel called, then follow your inner prompting. Rejecting society is another issue and you may want to look at that within yourself."

It was clear to me that this time working as a custodian was well spent, clarifying many aspects of my ego. I developed a deep appreciation for people who did this type of work or who were forced to do this type of work. One big lesson that dawned while spending all this time cleaning was that being connected to the Universe has nothing to do with external appearances. There is no mask, no image that makes one person more inwardly powerful than another. The custodian, the sewer cleaner, the dishwasher, the yard worker, the nurse, the doctor, the lawyer, the psychologist, the mailman are all just masks and not one is more important than the other. Not one person is more spiritual than the other, not one more worthy than the other; everyone and anyone can reach unending heights within themselves and no one would know, no one can know, and no one needs to know.

There is no way to tell how connected anyone is on the inside, and as they go along their day-to-day duties, whether sweeping hotels, doing surgeries, or picking fruit, only those who are connected will truly experience themselves. Being connected to the light within is not the same as dressing a certain way, having a certain name, or doing a certain ritual. I attempted to communicate all of what I was learning to Mathias. He just listened and nodded.

"We all have our path, and every individual's path is beautiful when given the chance to shine," he said.

* * *

After about a year and a half, I felt inwardly that I had learned what I needed to. I didn't feel reactive or shameful when people talked down to me or ignored me. I felt at peace in the role.

Around this time, I started to receive some inner guidance when meditating and I had dreams about what I should do next. I then enrolled in a massage college. The dreams clarified how I could integrate the many years of light work I had done with Okami and Mathias into a practice of healing with energy and the body.

CHAPTER TWENTY
THE GOLDEN FLAME

Mathias contacted me to meet him at his home on a certain date. The lower level of the home had become such a familiar place. As always, Vincente and Luciano were there to greet me. My love for those two dogs was so strong. I could see in Mathias's eyes that something powerful was going to happen.

He had me sit and said, "In many spiritual traditions around the world there is a moment when everything becomes light, and usually this moment of light is after you have faced your death. The doorway between this life and the transition is held by gold." I told him I didn't quite understand what he was saying.

He said, "It will make sense shortly." He had me close my eyes and then led me into meditation.

He said, "Take a deep breath, breathing in light and love, and just release any tension and stress. As you sink deeper, allow the love to build and send that love above you, receiving a beautiful white light in return, and then send that love below you to the center of the earth, seeing a beautiful light return. Feel how much you are loved. Breathe deep and center in your third eye. Now see your screen and surround yourself with a bubble of healing light and love, always surrounding you."

He continued, "Now I want you to sink deep down into yourself, down into your healing plane and see your lapis lazuli cave there and call on your animal ally, seeing it turn to light and merge with you. Feel the power and let your ally go. Now see the four elements as lights approaching and merge with them, feeling their light go wherever you need, merging, becoming one with the elements.

"Now see yourself come back up to your third eye center and I want you to now slowly travel upward, as if getting on an elevator, traveling up, up, up, to a beautiful healing plane above, where the teachers of the ages dwell. Notice the golden hue as you approach. I want you to reach that plane and be in that heightened place.

"Notice this incredible plane of healing. Notice the colors, the beautiful environment. Now, I want you to see a person or people slowly approaching you there. Watch as these beings approach. They are the masters above this world, the masters within and without. They are ever-present but above and beyond. I want you to connect and see the masters from above, talk to them, engage with them, ask them questions, and listen to what they have to say."

After staying quiet for some time, he continued, "Now see these masters of the Self become brighter, slowly turning into the most brilliant lights you have ever perceived, brighter and brighter, and see their lights merge into you. Feel the light of the masters, however that looks to you, whatever masters are there for you. Take in the light, as much as you need, and let them shower their grace on you, through you, within you. See the light of their endless wisdom and brilliance enhance and beautify you. Feel this experience, allowing their wisdom to be transmitted to you in energy form…

"Now let the energy go, feeling deep reverence and gratitude. I want you to see a cave to the side, a golden-colored cave. I want you to enter that cave. Sit in this cave with the masters either by your side or outside the cave. See a screen and a beautiful gold flame. The flame is dancing in the middle of the cave. Take that flame and brighten your body, transforming any darkness. Feel its power, feel its effects as you become golden and unified.

"Now I want you to see on that screen a negative personal belief you carry in this life. And not just this life – see it throughout many of your past lives. This is a belief that you have carried, and it has gotten stuck. This energetic belief about yourself is deep, deeper than this life, deeper than your past lives. This is a causal-level belief that is not in alignment and not needed anymore. See this belief arise on the screen and see how this belief has been impacting you in your emotions, in your mind, and in your body. See how it is not in alignment with your higher potential. See the golden fire build and start to transform that soul-level belief until it disappears in the sparks of the flame. Now after burning all of this energy that keeps you locked in, see only gold light left. A gold light of unity… This is the center point of all spiritual traditions and mysticism. This can be called a mystic flame."

He stayed quiet for a long time, letting me experience the power and transformation.

"Good. Now thank the energy and come back down while still being in that cave, bringing that beautiful golden light with you, as you. With deep gratitude, thank the masters who came to you. See yourself centered in your third eye, as a golden new being. There is a new center point within yourself. A point within yourself where all teachings meet…" There was a long pause.

He trailed his voice off with, "Everything is within you."

It took a very long time for me to come out of meditation. When I finally opened my eyes, he asked how that had gone for me.

I told him, "It was deeply profound. I saw teachers and healers who had been looking down on me for a long time. They were dressed in brilliant clothing, from many ancient and present traditions, exuding incredible light. They told me that it was important to simply practice and simply love. They showed me that there are multiple layers and planes of existence above and then they showed me there are equally beautiful reflections of these planes below in the earth, rich with deep colors and beyond human understanding. They can only be experienced, not logically explained. They said I was just scratching the surface."

I continued, "They then showed me that all these planes and all the masters were simply my own universal Self in multicolored clothing."

At this point, Mathias smiled and said, "Yes, they are guides on a new level and will start teaching you all sorts of new things. The whole idea is that you learn for yourself, from yourself, with a capital S."

He added, "These things I am sharing with you are only gateways; the true teachers are within you and will guide you always on your path. And in honesty at this point, you don't really need me to share these tools." He stopped talking and looked off into the distance.

He stayed quiet for a long time. He then held out his hand and as he had done before he traced a four-dimensional diamond in his hand. He said, "Many traditions around the world have texts that talk about the transition from life to death. There are texts like The Tibetan Book of Living and Dying that show the transition into the pure light of the Self."

While pointing to each corner of the diamond in his hand, he said, "When looking at the four directions we can see universal energy. Imagine the four energies of the East, West, North, and South, as well as the energies above and below, forming a diamond of pure light. We can see these pure lights in any tradition, whether it be Buddha, Krishna, Christ, Allah, or Earth itself. Light is universal and this gold light we are working with is a new doorway, helping you to be even more present in the here and now. This is a place of purer beingness and standing in this light creates a strong doorway between worlds."

At this point, I started to feel a bit overwhelmed. I had personal issues with religion and didn't want anything to do with certain religions due to past aggressive Christians trying to convert me. I hated the way people used the crucifix as a baseball bat and I started to squirm a bit in my seat.

Mathias saw my discomfort and reading the air said that the discomfort I felt was actually a good place for the gold flame healing.

He then looked at me with a mischievous smile, pushing something deeper. "It might be good to read the Bible... As well as the Torah, Quran, and any other religious text that you might be drawn to." His piercing eyes pushing on something deep within me.

He looked off in space and said, "They may just reveal their secrets that lie hidden under the generations of dross, generations of pain that exist in you and that exist in the world...

"Generations of pain have been inflicted by religion. The light we are accessing is beyond religion, beyond groups, beyond anything organized. And it is accessed individually, within oneself, by doing your own work. All the teachers of the past, they simply just did the work. But to be free enough to get past these traumas that exist within your multidimensional being, you must have the courage to face them head-on…"

He then raised his voice a bit. "Not everyone wants or desires to have that type of courage."

As I was walking out of Mathias's house, he stopped me, still noticing my discomfort. "Find the centerpiece of light within all religions, and then see yourself as the centerpiece of them, in the heart of everything."

I spent a lot of time with the golden flame. It sped up the work of the past-life clearing and helped me get straight to deep issues that existed beyond form. As I did this on the inside, I began reading religious books as recommended by Mathias.

I started with the Bible. At first, I found myself extremely averse to the things that I was reading. The stories that were so strange and aggressive felt ridiculous to me. Many were so harsh, especially in the Old Testament; yet what stood out to me most in the Bible was the life of Jesus. It ended up being nothing like anyone had ever preached to me. He was a man opposed to the lunacy of structure and oppressive religion. It was pretty clear to me that Jesus was like a wandering monk and his message was simply love. It blew my mind that generations of pain and war had been raged based on this book. Mathias was right that I would heal a lot by reading this book. I felt I could see Jesus and have my own view of him. I read sections of the Bible every day, meditated, and then put the energy into the gold flame.

I read the Torah, Talmud, and Quran using the same process. What I found amazing after reading these books was their similarity to one another. They overlapped and sounded similar in so many places. Sometimes I found the reading so dense and heavy that I would literally get a piercing headache, but I took it as a challenge for my ego to at least get through them.

At one point while finishing the Quran I meditated and saw these main books of Islam, Christianity, and Judaism in my mind. I saw that they were basically the same at the core; their message was the same with a varied color and light. In the meditation, I felt the books fall away but the message of light of these three Abrahamic religions remained. It was like looking at three faces of the same mountain. I eventually saw myself as one with the messages in the light, without the structure and without the dross. I could see so many lives lost, so much pain, for no reason. The underlying message of love was always there, so easily accessible, and all this generational pain was so pointless. The simplicity of the light and love behind the messages in the book was now so easy for me to see and experience.

This instigated within me a journey and exploration of more world religions. I read every religious text I got my hands on, such as the Dhammapada and other Buddhist sutras, and Buddhist books about higher beings such as the Earth Store Bodhisattva, a bodhisattva who is dedicated to the liberation of all human beings, particularly those stuck in hell. I delved into many texts of Hindu origins such as the Upanishads, Vedas, Yoga Sutras, Bhagavad Gita, and Ramayana. I studied the beautiful Guru Granth Sahib of Sikhism. I looked for any text I could get my hands on. I would read it, and then meditate on my reading, always seeing the light build while the form of the books just fell away. I would embrace a unifying light and feel oneness with the teachings. It was always clear that the goal was to experience these things as simple light. Over time I started to develop a great respect for the transmissions relayed, always with the energetic understanding of how much pain these books had created through misunderstanding.

This slowly led me to look for living teachers in many of these traditions. I looked for as many as I could find with the time I had to explore. I met Buddhist nuns and spent time meditating with them and listening to their talks in their nunnery. I connected with Zen monks from Taiwan and delved deep into their meditations and rituals, spending time in their silent meditations, rituals, and chanting. They gave me the name Chuan Shi, which translates to "Reality," after initiating me in the Three Refuges, the Three Gems of the Buddha, Dharma, and Sangha.

As time went on, I meditated with Buddhist monks from South Korea, Thailand, Japan, many Tibetan lineages, and more. I drank deeply from their teachings, transmission, and wisdom. I learned Vipassana, Zen, Loving-Kindness, Walking Meditation, Tonglen, and others. When spending time with monks I was always deeply inspired by their intense dedication to their individual faiths. Yet, underlying all these experiences was Mathias's teachings, always helping me find the unity of light that existed underneath.

At one point I ended up at a celebration of a nine-foot-tall Buddha carved out of a huge piece of Jade from New Zealand. Buddhist monks from all over the area and from many countries and different lineages came to see it. Watching the streams of different-colored robes, I meditated under the green Buddha for many days in silence opening my eyes to watch thousands honor it with different mantras, prayers, and celebrations. As members of each sect did their individual rituals, they were different flavors but all one in devotion. Again and again I was seeing a beautiful underlying light of unity in all the rituals.

Later I sought out Hindu lineages, monks, and those considered enlightened and I practiced meditations with them, spending endless amounts of time meditating with them. One teacher from South India told me to form meditation groups and initiate people with sacred ash on their third eye. I was taught so many varying fashions of meditation, from simple to complex. One woman, considered a saint and incarnation of the Goddess, gave me the name Gaurish, a name of Shiva. Later, I was told that she gave names of Shiva to people who were meditators. I went to Sikh and Hindu temples, sang devotional music, chanted Sanskrit, and met swamis that exhibited powers that can't be explained by today's science.

In the end, all these varied practices and teachers would unify, turn to light, and fall away within me. Over time I saw there was so much unity between monks within the depths of different faiths. A friend one day approached me and told me this quote from the poet Rumi: "All these religions, all this singing, one song."

As I studied each religion and really delved into the honey of each teaching, I found myself drawn in by its specific mystical teachers, and each time I would find someone wholly dedicated to its teachings. I always found myself wanting to give it my all.

At one point I asked a Buddhist monk about becoming a monk, and I asked a Hindu monk about becoming a monk. I started the process for one and then the other, and each time some unexpected circumstance arose that prevented me from going further, So, I fell away from becoming a monk or renunciate.

Many times during my exploration of world religions I would go to my inner healing plane above and dialogue with my inner teachers. When I did this, I would clearly feel that the transmissions I got from the inside were in line with what I was learning on the outside. At this point in my life, it was normal for me to meditate for over five hours a day. I gave away my car and decided to walk or ride the bus everywhere as a way to simplify and discipline my life.

During my many years of studying world religions, I rarely connected with Mathias. On the rare occasions I did connect, I would share with him what I was doing and he would just listen. Strangely, each time I saw him I wanted him to be more interested in what I was experiencing. I found that over the years I started to slowly get upset with his lack of appreciation and acknowledgment of my experiences.

I thought to myself, "How could he not be interested in these amazing things I am doing?!" I had learned all these techniques and he never acted impressed or moved; he just listened. The less responsive he was, the more I became inwardly agitated and felt maybe he was jealous or judging me. This energy built any time I saw him and would arise from something deep inside me. I eventually spiraled myself into believing that maybe the work I had done with him wasn't as profound as I had thought. He would just sit quietly, listening. At one point, rejecting Mathias in my head, I felt he had nothing more profound to share. I left feeling resentful and decided that the work with him wasn't what I had thought it was. The emotional pressure built so intensely that I left and did not connect with him for many years.

During those years away from Mathias I spent time with endless spiritual groups and got involved with many different teachings. I became like a spiritual butterfly; I would never stay put and was always onto the next teaching. I would always get to a point where I felt a limit to the teachings I was learning; none of them truly satisfied me. I had an underlying thirst that I couldn't quench, but I searched endlessly.

At one point I was chanting countless Sanskrit mantras. I developed a daily practice of chanting the one thousand names of Devi, the Divine Mother, every morning, and then shifted to the 1000 names of Shiva, then Vishnu. This thirst that I couldn't quench became my obsession, an unending search for something better, bigger, brighter, more spiritually powerful. It was never enough. Slowly each external search would lose its shine and I would be off to the next spiritual practice, the next group, and the next teacher.

After many years of doing this type of exploring I eventually felt moved to go back and reconnect with Mathias. I went and visited with him. He was warm and listened as he always did. Again, he did not say much.

He then asked, "What did you learn from all the books, all the churches, temples, teachers, and all the monks?"

I stared at him for a long time. It was a simple question. I searched hard inside myself, but I could not answer. I saw all these actions I was doing but I couldn't say what I had learned from them.

His eyes extra shiny, looking at me he said, "You've done this so many lives, no?"

Somewhat reserved I said, "Yeah, it does all seem pretty familiar."

He said, "Are you wanting to play it out again in this life?"

I paused for a long time thinking about what he had just said. I could feel a pressure building in me, a deep, uncomfortable feeling. I attempted to write off what he was saying in frustration.

Anger was building and I wanted to contradict him, but something was starting to crack inside me. An awareness started slowly to release. I almost walked away again like I had done many years ago, but something was different. I now felt an intense amount of control in my body, in my mind, and I could see in my third eye that my energy was clenched around something hard in my heart. It appeared like a fist not wanting to let go, and I was going to do anything to fight to prevent myself from letting it go.

I didn't need to say anything. Mathias could see what I was experiencing. "What's inside that control?"

I felt my whole body clench as if turning to stone. I was sweating.

Then suddenly like a dam releasing, a cascade of images came over my third eye. I saw my life, life after life after life, lived as a monk. I saw myself taking vows of renunciation and celibacy in many different traditions. In these lives, I had intense and powerful self-control, the ability to control all my bodily desires with powers that developed from that self-control.

Yet, the control was similar and repetitive over many lives. Within each life an intense type of ego began building, a spiritual ego, built layer upon layer. This control existed with a desire for power. As this vision continued to build, I saw how in each life I thought that control and self-discipline were the best and the only way to reach spiritual heights. It was a deep, intense belief that control of the body was the one and only way to God. It was clear that the search and the goal were originally based on the search for Spirit in one form or another, but so many of those lives got sidetracked and lacked love as their basis. In so many lives I became mired in spiritual techniques, spiritual powers, transmissions, and in the mask of what a spiritual person was supposed to be.

As if he were also watching the scenes that were going on Mathias prodded, "What kind of ego was it that developed over those many lives?" He pushed it deeper.

I told him I saw that each life had a certain goal. One was to be the most sacrificial, another to be the most powerful, another to be the most spiritual. In one life I became a renunciate leader dressed all in orange, and a Catholic friar in another. The ego continued building, and I told myself life after life that this was the only way, the right way, and the best way. The more I saw, the more the images sped up, and the clearer it became that this duality had gotten patterned on my soul.

Mathias's gaze relaxed and he said, "This seems like a perfect time for that inner golden flame. You remember, don't you?"

The pressure was still in my body and so I closed my eyes and traveled inside myself to the gold cave and gold flame of unity. I saw all these lives in front of me and all the things I was doing in my current life, and I simply placed them in the flames. This weight and intensity I had carried for so long in my heart, burdens I had carried for so long, I just placed in the fire. I watched as they transformed, like a heavy weight I had not realized I had been dragging along my entire life. Endless beliefs burning in the fire, burning away spiritual beliefs that everything had to be accomplished through intense sacrifice, intense and deep religious ritual, and extreme self-control. I felt layers clear off me, layer after layer of belief, layer after layer of religious guilt merging into one golden flame.

I then saw each religion I had tried to become, each one I had tried to embody in those lives, become a brilliant dancing light. Those lights increased and merged with me, and I became one with them inside the centerpiece of the gold flame. This light grew and grew until it dissipated all the duality and it all became only one gold light.

As my view shifted I began to feel physically free of the pressure. I saw that all the work I had done over those many lives wasn't a waste but a lesson. I saw how necessary it was to my evolution. The difference now was that I could see it all as a choice, not a requirement, for spirituality. Renunciation was simply a choice, not a requirement, for being with one's inner self.

I then saw how this present life was a gift, and a time to try and be free of the spiritual ego by seeing that I was already free. At one point I saw myself doing endless prayers, dedicating myself to the bodhisattva way, which meant not being free until all beings were free. Yet what I realized in this moment of realization was that all beings are already free... We are always free... We are all Source. As this realization dawned great freedom came over my spirit as I saw that all beings are already free beyond their body, that suffering is an illusion. With this deep awareness, I slowly let myself float back down into the present moment in my body.

When I opened my eyes Mathias was looking off in space. He said, "There's nowhere you need to go, there's no one you need to be, there's nowhere you need to be but here with your Source... Fully embodied in the world, but not of it. Simply now.

"You can be all religions, you can be all spiritual traditions, yet you are beyond all of them. That is the key: embodied fully but free... This is a simple reality... This is simple freedom. This is the place of the mystic. To simply be love." Mathias looked off into space again and then quietly laughed to himself.

CHAPTER TWENTY-ONE
HOLDING THE WORLD

Over the many years when I would visit with Mathias, he would occasionally bring up the fact that he was just a teacher of tools. He once said, "I am no Guru. I definitely don't desire followers. I am simply here to give you the tools for your journey so that you can find your own path, your own power, your own magic, and answers."

He would laugh and relate his humanness and flaws and often mocked his own pattern of trying to control everything. He would talk about piercing personal darkness with humor.

"Laughter is the balm of the pain we create for ourselves. The more human we become, the more powerful we truly are," he said once.

One day when I was visiting with him he gave me a very serious look.

He said, "I once belonged to a spiritual group. This group had a leader that was very dynamic and exhibited many otherworldly powers. Her dynamism, her psychic abilities, and other dynamics drew many people around her. At one point while I was receiving teachings from this woman, I performed what many considered a miracle in front of her and her students. It wasn't intentional on my part but a simple energetic technique that I was taught. When I turned to see the look on the teacher's face, she was not smiling; rather she seemed upset. The more the other students of hers asked me about what I had done, the angrier she seemed to appear. After a few students approached me and asked how to do what I had done she turned to me and said, 'Your self-importance is showing to everyone. I gave you that power and I can take it away.'"

Mathias said he knew at that moment that he needed to get out of that group and fast. When he left, the teacher told all the students that he was a bad person and convinced all the students to stay away from him, not to socialize with him. Mathias said it was quite shocking to see the teacher try and have so much power and control. He was grateful he left the group. He realized later just how unbalanced the woman was and how that had endangered those around her.

He said, "I am bringing this up to you because you have an energetic tendency to give your power away."

He continued, "This previous teacher of mine gathered more and more students and more and more money. Intuitively I felt that originally she was tapped into something beautiful and even wholesome. As time went on the money and power influenced her teachings, eventually creating massive control dynamics on many subtle levels. This caused it to turn into a cult of immense magnitude."

He said, "She stopped doing her inner work, seeing her humanness, and got lost in the seduction of power."

Mathias said he was simply here to share tools that might help. He said he let Spirit choose the students and that the students approached him, not the other way around.

Sometimes I even got the feeling that Mathias didn't want to teach. He often mentioned that through meditation a person could gain any number of miraculous happenings, but these were often just distractions on the path toward inner healing and inner freedom. They were a natural result of going deeper within and an expansion of awareness.

Over the years I pondered upon these dynamics that he spoke of. I could see that Mathias had a certain detachment with his students as well as respect. I never once encountered a fellow student who felt he overstepped his role as a teacher. The students would filter in and out, but he definitely did not seem attached to them staying in his life. The times I saw events I considered miraculous, they always seemed like simple teaching moments.

As I did my own exploring with different spiritual groups, I found Mathias's words gave me perspective on the teacher, the meditator, or the group leader and how they used their position of power. Did they use it for service to others, or for some other reason? I often noticed whether the power they projected was in alignment with their words and actions. If their words, thoughts, and actions did not line up it would often become quite clear in their relationships with their students. If such a misalignment occurred, I would quickly see the projection on those around. This sometimes appeared as a lack of vulnerability and honesty and would be an indicator for me to move on. If a teacher told students what was wrong with them and blamed them for failures, that made me a little more present to their actions. I often bounced the teachers with Mathias inside my mind. I always appreciated Mathias's ability to speak of his experiences and share the tools without forcing his beliefs on me.

Since I had started this work at a young age it left me open to exploring many spiritual leaders, teachers, and groups. There was never an instance where I regretted learning from other teachers, and even if the group turned out to be unhealthy there was always something good to take from it. All the myriads of teachings and traditions were beautiful lights of different colors. Every teaching, no matter how bad, always provided a beneficial lesson in one way or another.

* * *

At this point in my life, I felt strong in my practice and my teachers were all prompted from within me. My meditations were guiding themselves. It had been many years since I had seen Mathias in person. I would occasionally connect with him in meditation. One day he popped up strongly in my mind, along with an inner message that it was time to complete something I had not finished. I felt the inner message so strongly that I went to The Sage to see him.

It had been a while and there was something different in the air. I knew deeply that something was about to change in our relationship. Over the length of my 20s and into my 30s I had experienced so much with Mathias, and yet it felt like it was time for a change. I walked into the alley to see him standing, staring at me, like he always was, an eagle looking down from the ledge, knowing I was coming.

He gave me a big smile and said, "I was expecting you."

I said, "Yes, though I am not sure I'm ready for this shift."

He said, "I have given you all the tools you need and so much more beyond that. I have given you all I can."

He looked at me and said, "One more lesson before liftoff?"

I felt some tears well up in my eyes. Since I was 18 years old Mathias had been a mentor, a guide, a healer, and a teacher to me. Though not always there, in physical form, he had assisted in my life without abandon and with utmost care. My gratitude was endless.

He held out his hand, and like times in the past he traced the 3-dimensional diamond and said, "Now, in all traditions, in all the lands, you can use this diamond and its light. This is the work we have been brought together to do. Imagine any spiritual form, guide, or energy in the diamond and it will work universally across cultures and across the light spectrum."

As he pointed to each corner of the diamond he said, "Like I've said in the past, see the Buddha in the South, see the Buddha in the North, in the East, in the West, the Buddha above, and the Buddha below. See the light of the Buddha form a complete diamond. See the element of earth as Buddha, the Buddha of water, fire, and the air. See the Buddha in each rainbow color, as the red light, then the orange, all the way to the purple. See the Buddha as the three healing flames, the white flame of this life, the lapis lazuli flame of the dream plane, and see the Buddha as the causal gold flame of unity. See it all as the Buddha in all ways, one brilliant light. See the Buddha as you merge into a brilliant oneness in the center of your heart or mind.

"Any tradition will work with this. See Allah as the source of the North, South, East, West, Above, and Below. See Allah as the rainbow and the elements, the healing flames. See Allah as the centerpiece of all animals and as all the masters above."

He looked at me and said, "See Allah as every multiplane reality you can travel to. Now see Jesus in the same way, the Orishas the same, Krishna the same, Great Spirit the same. See Quan Yin, Devi, or Tara in the four directions, above and below. See Mother Mary as the very light of yourself, Lakshmi, any form of the Divine Mother, any master, any form of God, any symbol, any word, any energy, any anti-energy. You can move into any of these energies at any moment in time. Or, you can choose to experience emptiness in all directions. See all these energies as your very own Self — above, below, in all directions, as oneness. You are all of it; you are one light in all directions. It is all simply you, this whole inner-outer reality.

"The more you hold those lights for yourself, surrender, explore, and understand them, the more you can relate to others' experiences. Spirit will move your diamond to reflect those who need it, and this could look completely different for each individual you work with.

"Allow the moment to move you, and the work you share with others will automatically be in alignment. You are the centerpiece of any and all beliefs in all of creation. They are your very own self." He then stayed quiet for a long time, staring off in space. I interrupted the silence. "I understand... I feel it..." He nodded as if pushing me to say more.

I said, "I am the light of love in all directions, in all creation, in all possibilities, in the diamond and beyond. I am the love from past to future. I am the love that permeates all universal energy. I am the silence that exists beyond the light. I am everything and I am nothing. I am the love beyond all time and space. I am that."

Mathias looked at me and said. "Many people can say this, but the key here is that you are experiencing it. You have experienced it because you have done the work, the meditation, and the healing. Words mean little but you have experienced this throughout your inner world and meditation."

And then like a dawning realization, a deep sense of awe came over me — absolute awe. At that moment I realized all this work with Mathias had simply helped me to embody my near-death experience, this experience that I had so long ago. At that moment I had the full feeling and perception of being fully in my body, yet fully awake in that experience of endless love within. The goal of all the work with Mathias was to reach that space and be able, even in the slightest, to touch that endless space of love in my day-today life. Here I was, feeling it in the here and now. I was amazed. I always knew I had never really lost it; no one ever really loses it, but paradoxically I couldn't see myself as it.

The gratitude that poured over me in that moment was incredible. This man had so selflessly dedicated so much of his life and time to me. Not just him but Okami and others. I could never repay them. They didn't seem real; it felt like a dream. I could never repay the healing, the power that was instilled in me.

Mathias was looking at me, smiling. Reading my mind he said, "You don't need to repay me. If you choose to serve then you can offer to others what I have offered to you, but Spirit gives freely of itself like all of nature. Earth and Sky never ask for anything in return."

He patted my back and he said, "Now that we are here, there appears to be a new crossroads ahead."

I said, "Well, all I have really ever wanted was to help other people."

He said, "I know… Tell me, Andrew, what does that look like to you?"

I said, "Someday I would like to teach as you have taught me."

At that moment two large crows came hopping into the alley cawing loudly, breaking the continuity of our conversation. They stopped hopping and both appeared to be looking at me. Mathias laughed and said, "Well you got someone's attention." I got quiet inside and spoke to them within myself.

"Well, it sounds like you'd better get to work!" Mathias said laughing, breaking me from my crow conversation.

He said, "There is a group of colleagues I belong to. We meet on rare occasions, only when drawn together by Spirit. We just happen to be meeting next week. It's a small group of teachers that meditate on world events. We are called to hold the world together.

"Becoming a teacher is not something someone else can give; it is something that happens within oneself at an individual's own time. If you wish to be around other teachers, then come to this meeting of colleagues. We are all just colleagues on this journey together."

I could feel a certain intensity in making the decision to be around only teachers, a certain letting go of the student/teacher relationship with Mathias. After so many years of practicing this work, I realized there was a certain maturity that would need to be maintained if I were to become a teacher – a new level of being connected to myself, taking guidance alone, leaning on no one else but my inner Self for that guidance. Deep down I knew it was time. It had been time for a while.

As my heart and mind slowly came into sync, I thought to myself, "What greater gift could I give to others?"

The answer to myself was, "There is no greater gift to give others than to share freedom."

Mathias then said, "In this group, we meditate on world events… We hold the world, understanding we are the world… We heal the world, understanding we are the world… We heal ourselves because we are the world."

I gave a half-smile and said, "It looks like my work has just begun."

ABOUT THE AUTHOR

Andrew Zorich is an international teacher of integrated bodywork, meditation, and self-healing. He has a private practice located in Seattle, Washington.

www.DiamondBodywork.com

Made in the USA
Coppell, TX
31 July 2020